Earth, My Likeness

Earth, My Likeness

Nature Poetry of **Walt Whitman**

Edited by Howard Nelson

North Atlantic Books
Berkeley, California

Published by   and   Heron Dance Art Studio
North Atlantic Books   Hummingbird Lane
P.O. Box 12327   179 Rotax Road
Berkeley, California 94712   North Ferrisburgh, Vermont 05473
                                                 888-304-3766
Cover and interior art by Roderick MacIver   www.herondance.org
Cover and book design by Brad Greene
Printed in the United States of America

Earth, My Likeness: Nature Poetry of Walt Whitman is sponsored by the Society for the Study of Native Arts and Sciences, a nonprofit educational corporation whose goals are to develop an educational and cross-cultural perspective linking various scientific, social, and artistic fields; to nurture a holistic view of arts, sciences, humanities, and healing; and to publish and distribute literature on the relationship of mind, body, and nature.

North Atlantic Books' publications are available through most bookstores. For further information, visit our Web site at www.northatlanticbooks.com or call 800-733-3000.

Library of Congress Cataloging-in-Publication Data

Whitman, Walt, 1819–1892.
    Earth, my likeness : nature poetry of Walt Whitman / edited by
Howard Nelson.
        p. cm.
    Summary: "Earth, My Likeness is a collection of poetry by Walt Whitman that focuses on nature and contains much of his best and most vital work accompanied by beautiful watercolor illustrations"—Provided by publisher.
    Originally published: N. Ferrisburg, Vt. : Heron Dance Press, 2006.
    ISBN 978-1-55643-910-0
    1. Nature—Poetry. I. Nelson, Howard, 1947- II. Title.
    PS3204.N45 2010
    811.3—dc22
                                                   2009036814

1 2 3 4 5 6 7 8 9 UNITED 15 14 13 12 11 10

One day Whitman insisted on holding [Horace] Traubel's very cold hand when he arrived: "It is cold, therefore I keep it. It is a reminiscence of the open air, the sky, the sea, and no one knows how precious these are—have been—to me. And indeed, it is to surcharge *Leaves of Grass* with them that was my presiding spinal purpose from the start."

> —— From *Intimate with Walt: Selections from Whitman's Conversations with Horace Traubel,* 1888–1892, edited by Gary Schmidgall

Inside the outer bars or beach this south bay is everywhere comparatively shallow; of cold winters all thick ice on the surface. As a boy I often went forth with a chum or two, on those frozen fields, with hand-sled, axe and eel-spear, after messes of eels. We would cut holes in the ice, sometimes making quite an eel-bonanza, and filling our baskets with great, fat, sweet, white-meated fellows. The scenes, the ice, drawing the hand-sled, cutting holes, spearing the eels, &c., were of course just such fun as is dearest to boyhood. The shores of this bay, winter and summer, and my doings there in early life, are woven all through L. of G.

> —From "Paumanok, and My Life on It as Child and Young Man," *Specimen Days*

I believe whatever happens, I shall not forget this earth.

> —Walt Whitman

Notes on the Text

In the original version of this book, published by Heron Dance Press, I worked from *Leaves of Grass: Comprehensive Reader's Edition*, edited by Harold W. Blodgett and Sculley Bradley (New York University Press, 1965) and the Dover Publications edition of *Specimen Days* (1995). In preparing this new and expanded edition, I have relied on the Library of America's *Walt Whitman: Complete Poetry and Collected Prose*, edited by Justin Kaplan (1982), now the most readily available authoritative presentation of Whitman. The quotations from John Burroughs are taken from *Whitman in His Own Time*, edited by Joel Myerson (University of Iowa Press, 1991).

Whitman was an inveterate reviser, sometimes for better, sometimes not. The textual variations are sometimes fascinating, and those wanting to check them should see *Walt Whitman—Selected Poems 1855–1892*, edited by Gary Schmidgall (St. Martin's Press, 1999), which presents the poems in earlier versions. Whitman scholarship is a very active field, but the three works by Schmidgall cited in this introduction represent an enormous outpouring of scholarly energy and intelligence and deserve to be singled out. I am indebted to many Whitman scholars whose work has informed my understanding of Whitman and his work. A particularly useful critical source is *Walt Whitman: An Encyclopedia*, edited by J. R. LeMaster and Donald Kummings (Garland Publishing, 1998), which is comprehensive and concise at the same time, a rich gathering of information and interpretation from Whitman scholars from across the country and the world.

I resisted the temptation to give titles to selections that are excerpts from longer works, but I suggest that they be read as poems that are something a little different from what they are in their original contexts, and that stand by themselves. Of course, the reader should look to the poems as they appear in *Leaves of Grass* itself, but I'll admit to having taken great pleasure in disassembling and rearranging what Walt Whitman so painstakingly created in his life-long book, and in joining the selections from the poetry with what I consider the prose poetry of *Specimen Days*. I hope Whitman would be open to the project. Being in the company of his work and the life it contains has been the deepest pleasure and nourishment. I am grateful to him every day.

Contents

Introduction

WALT WHITMAN'S nature poetry is unlike that of any other poet. Though he has been much imitated and emulated, no one else's poems sound or feel like his. Why this is so is hard to say exactly, but the flow of his long lines, the sharpness and sometimes quirkiness of his imagery, and his abundant pleasure in being alive come together into an immediacy that is not only distinctive but that really does feel natural. It is art, of course, not a river or ocean waves. But when he is at his best, he has a way of putting us into a natural place with all its freshness. Poetry in the nineteenth century favored a formal approach and tone, and when Whitman came on the scene his work struck some as dazzling, some as bewildering, and others as outrageous. There were many reasons for this, but I think that each of those reactions was due in part to a feeling in his readers that they were having an experience in his poems that had more to do with nature than literature. They were not used to poems being this fluid and wet, or having so much open air.

Whitman's book *Leaves of Grass* was the work of decades. From the age of thirty-seven on, he kept his title, adding new poems and reorganizing and fine-tuning from edition to edition. The end result is a book as daunting as the Bible, to which Whitman compared it. Approaching *Leaves of Grass* can be like trying to embrace a sequoia. In focusing on his nature poetry, we won't get all of him, but we do get a crucial part that is deeply connected to all that Whitman was and wrote. We will also be reading some of his best and most beautiful work.

While Whitman gave us some of the most vibrant nature poetry we have, it should be acknowledged that he is also the author of one of the most awful nature poems ever written. That would be "Song of the Redwood-Tree," which combines a highly oratorical tone with a dose of nineteenth-century boosterism of modern progress that is likely to make twenty-first-century readers wince. In the poem Whitman accepts and even celebrates the destruction of the big trees, as they make room for "the flashing and golden pageant of California . . . / Lands bathed in sweeter, rarer, healthier air . . ." and for "a swarming and busy race settling and organizing everywhere." Given the air pollution and sprawl that have turned out to be so much a part of the pageant of California, and of so many other places, the poem takes on a huge irony. Whitman has the tree speak, encouraging its fellow redwoods to accept their fate: "With Nature's calm content, with tacit huge delight . . . / For a superber race . . . / For them we abdicate." The critic M. Jimmie Killingsworth, in his book *Walt Whitman and the Earth,* suggests that when Whitman wrote the poem he was depressed and on the verge of giving up, and that he projected this state of mind onto the redwood. True as this may be, it doesn't make the poem any easier to like. One wants to say, "Stop, Walt, please . . ."

Of course, there's always some unfairness in holding ancestors up to contemporary awareness. Even extraordinary people like Whitman, or Abraham Lincoln, were products of their time, and for all their genius or wisdom, they sometimes disappoint us. (We, meanwhile, are unaware of what limitations and flaws our own attitudes may reveal to people a century or so from now.) Still, there's a point to be made here beyond that Whitman had blind spots, or that his work was uneven. That is, he was not a conservationist. Whitman belonged to a time when the earth, even a single continent, still seemed infinite to most people. Conservationists weren't very common in Whitman's time, but John Muir was only twenty years younger, and Thoreau was of his exact generation. Thoreau stood in opposition to his society's dominant values of business, expansion, and devotion to technology, and in solidarity with the natural world. Whitman, while he was political and capable of telling attacks on conventional society, was inside the social pulse in a way that Thoreau was not. He embraced the materialism and technology of his age. Thoreau's comments in *Walden* about the railroad are a classic meditation on the relative advantages and costs of technology, and of what is usually thought of as progress. Whitman, on the other hand, wrote an admiring and excited poem called "To a Locomotive in Winter." Thoreau—even from childhood, according to relatives—was one to judge. Whitman was more accepting—of people, and of the world in all its abundance and confusion.

Thoreau, the naturalist, the critic; Whitman, the celebrant, the democrat—different, yet with deep currents in common. What they had in common has been known as transcendentalism, which included the beliefs that the physical world is also spiritual, and that human beings may yet become something more than we generally are. As they are two of the greatest embodiments of individualism that ever were, it's interesting to think of them together. They actually were together once, but no great conversation resulted. Thoreau, impressed with Whitman's poetry, went to Brooklyn to meet him. They sat together in the modest, somewhat disheveled, working-class room that Whitman shared with his mentally disabled brother—quite different quarters from the famous, fastidiously simple cabin by the pond. They talked a little, but later when Thoreau's companion, Bronson Alcott, described the meeting, he said, "Each seemed planted fast in reserves, surveying the other curiously, like two beasts, each wondering what the other would do, whether to snap or run, and it came to no more than cold compliments between the two." Perhaps we can see in this brief encounter not only a meeting of two great American writers, but also an early image of two kinds of environmentalist—the pure and the impure, the one that sees human beings as the problem and the one that sees them as part of nature—trying to figure out what to say to one another. It's a scenario that's been acted out in thousands of variations since then. Between the two, we might have the makings of a synthesis, and personally I think we need both of their perspectives as we try to arrive at a viable environmental wisdom.

Years later, when Whitman visited Concord, he went to Thoreau's grave (and Hawthorne's, lying close by) and to Walden Pond. One of the homage stones in the cairn near the site of Thoreau's cabin was placed there by Whitman.

If Whitman wasn't a conservationist, what was he? We could call him an ecologist, if we consider the root meaning of the word, which is "house" or "home." Whitman wanted us to feel at home in our bodies and on the earth, and few writers match him in communicating that feeling. He himself was a robust, casual, observant human animal, with great warmth—sometimes expressed openly, sometimes held in, as what he referred to as "subtle electric fire." Speaking of his work as a volunteer aide in army hospitals during the Civil War, Whitman said, "I fancy the reason I am able to do some good in the hospitals, among the poor languishing and wounded boys, is that I am so large and well—indeed like a great wild buffalo, with much hair—many of the soldiers are from the west, and far north—and they take to a man who has not the bleached shiny and shaved cut of the cities of the east." There was a kind of animal magnetism in Whitman that many felt and responded to—felt in his person, felt in his poetry. One woman, Anne Gilchrist, fell in love with him from reading his poetry and traveled from England hoping to marry him. Whitman, not much romantically inclined toward women, didn't encourage her, but she came. Though it didn't work out as she wished, they became friends anyway.

In a number of places in his work Whitman expresses his admiration of animals and longs to be more like them. They seem to him solid, at one with themselves, "placid and self-contain'd." But it wasn't only in animals that he saw the vitality and aplomb he liked. He saw the same qualities in certain human beings. Sometimes, wandering around looking with his sharp and luminous eyes, he saw many people who seemed to him as graceful and as at-home

Earth, My Likeness

on the earth as healthy animals. Look at some of the photographs of Whitman and you will see what I mean about his eyes. Reading his poems, for instance the catalogues of images jotted one after another, you can see that his eyes were sharp and luminous not only in their look but in their seeing as well.

Whitman didn't draw the hard line between human and animal that means so much to some people. The idea of evolution was fine with him. Even before Darwin's *The Origin of Species* was published, Whitman had a vision of the continuum of life through vast stretches of time. He was one who could see easily, you might say naturally, through the idea that the earth was only a few thousand years old. For him, it was a sort of personal experience:

> *We have thus far exhausted trillions of winters and summers,*
> *There are trillions ahead, and trillions ahead of them....*
> *Afar down I see the huge first Nothing, I know I was even there,*
> *I waited unseen and always, and slept through the lethargic mist,*
> *And took my time, and took no hurt from the fetid carbon.*
> *Long I was hugg'd close—long and long.*

Certain people seemed to him to be specimens of what it means to be fully alive, vibrant and completely natural. He noticed these qualities especially in working men, but he saw it in women too. It might be a woman in some domestic routine, something as simple as setting plates calmly on the table for dinner, but he also liked to think of a woman leaving the house and going to swim in the river. He envisioned a world in which women are "tann'd in the face by shining suns and blowing winds, / Their flesh has the old divine suppleness and strength, / They know how to swim, row, ride, wrestle, shoot, run, strike, retreat, advance, resist, defend themselves...." Not all of Whitman's hopeful prophecies have worked out as he imagined them, but this is one that has largely come true.

As I was rereading *Leaves of Grass* to create this collection, I found it enjoyably difficult to know exactly what my definition of nature poetry should be. In "Give Me the Splendid Silent Sun," Whitman says that he likes the city at least as much as the country, human faces perhaps most of all. I decided on a liberal conception. Whitman liked the phrase "natural persons," and it could be that nothing is more central to his vision than seeing human beings as every bit as natural as an oak tree or a warbling bird. The presence of the oak, the singing of a mockingbird, the calm of cattle swishing their tails in the shade—these are things that he aspires to. "I think I could turn and live with animals," he says. At times, animals seem preferable to people: "They do not sweat and whine about their condition, / They do not lie awake in the dark and weep for their sins, / They do not make me sick discussing their duty to God, / Not one is dissatisfied, not one is demented with the mania of owning things." But Whitman's thrust is to honor both nonhuman and human animals, and I've tried to embody that sense in this collection. I've gone a little further than that, broadening the conception of "natural persons" by including a couple of Whitman's sketches of humanity when it is not radiating exuberance or well-being: his description of Abraham Lincoln during the war, and another of a tramp family, some of the nineteenth century's homeless, living close to nature in a different and difficult way. In this broader sense, the sadness in Lincoln's eyes and the haunted look of a poor young woman are part of nature too. Whitman was an ecstatic, but he knew very well that it isn't all loafing on the grass on a transparent summer morning. He is a great poet of exuberance, and he is a great poet of grief, and in both cases, the natural world is woven into his singing. When he comes to write an elegy for Lincoln, he turns to the natural world for his imagery and for his means of mourning, to green and growing things, as can be seen in the excerpts from "When Lilacs Last in the Dooryard Bloom'd," included in the group of poems I've called "Herbage and Comrades." In his physical life, his spiritual life, and his poetic vocabulary, Whitman's connection to the natural world was fundamental.

I've mentioned Thoreau as a sort of complement to Whitman, and there's another of his contemporaries I'd like to mention as well. The 1850s were an amazing decade in American literature, producing not only *Leaves of Grass* and *Walden*, but also *Moby Dick*. In a way, the story of Ahab is a subplot in the book's larger story, which is nature itself, contemplated through Melville's surrogate, Ishmael, whose consciousness is one of the great intuitive, funny, poetic treasures of literature. When asked to make a list of outstanding works in the history of nature writing, Annie Dillard gave a one-sentence comment on *Moby Dick:* "The best book ever written about nature." Some readers find the chapters on whales overbearing and digressive, but to others they are the most wonderful part, where "the great flood-gates of the wonder-world [swing] open"—whales, the ocean, nature itself.

I bring in Melville because these three writers seem to belong together not only in the timing of their births and their greatest creative work, and not only as nature writers, but more particularly as water writers. Thoreau is the pond man par excellence, and the way he knows Walden Pond—its temperatures and depths, its fish and underwater sights, its boundaries and surrounding land, with limits at the same time it is infinite—is in keeping with the carefulness and clarity of his personality. Melville, on the other hand, is the ocean writer, the contemplator of whales and thousands of miles of water where there is no shore—and who knows where the bottom is? And Whitman? He is the writer of the places where water and land meet—seashore, creek and riverbank; river-crossings on ferries, wading in surf, swimming from beaches. Just as the pond expresses Thoreau's mind and the ocean Melville's, the water's edge expresses Whitman. In his poems we are very often in the place where we feel both the concrete immediacy of the here and now and the flux of time and eternity. On a ferry he leans on a solid rail stock-still, enjoying the sun and air, realizing at the same time that what is under and around him is all a flow.

There's no record that Whitman and Melville ever met, but it's possible that they saw each other. The opening chapter of *Moby Dick*, "Loomings," is one of the best essays ever written about water. Melville beautifully captures the attraction of the human mind and soul to water; it is something instinctual, almost magical. He says, in a sentence that is a sort of one-line poem, "Yes, as we all know, meditation and water are wedded forever." In this chapter he describes walking the shore of Manhattan on a Sunday afternoon and seeing multitudes of water-gazers "posted like silent sentinels all around the town": "But look!

Here come more crowds, pacing straight for the water, and seemingly bound for a dive. Strange! Nothing will content them but the extremest limit of the land; loitering under the shady lee of yonder warehouses will not suffice. No, they must get just as nigh the water as they possibly can without falling in."

One of those water-gazers that Melville observed might have been Whitman. He often wandered around Manhattan, and was drawn to the island's edges. He looked into the river and said, "Flood-tide below me! I see you face to face." On the other hand, if Whitman was one of the crowd heading for the water, he might not have stopped and stood transfixed in a reverie of water-contemplation. Just as likely, he would have been swimming, or watching the boys diving from the docks. In his days as a newspaperman, he wrote editorials praising the freedom and healthiness of such bathing, and he protested official attempts to prevent it. When he wasn't in Manhattan, Whitman was often out on the beaches of Long Island (or Paumanok, as he liked to call it, using the Native American name) taking long barefoot walks on the sand, or reciting Homer to the waves.

He loved to ramble on the seashore. As Killingsworth says, it was a sacred place for him, "most certainly the site of the soul's first on-set and deepest revelations... a site of survival, to which the poet returns again and again to reconnect with the earth and regenerate his energy." As a casual reminiscence, the sacredness of the seashore sounds like this:

> Many a good day or half-day did I have, wandering through those solitary cross-roads, inhaling the peculiar and wild aroma. Here, and all along the island and its shores, I spent intervals many years, all seasons, sometimes riding, sometimes boating, but generally afoot, (I was always then a good walker,) absorbing fields, shores, marine incidents, characters, the bay-men, farmers, pilots—always had a plentiful acquaintance with the latter, and with fishermen—went every

summer on sailing trips—always liked the bare sea-beach, south side, and have some of my happiest hours on it to this day.

As I write, the whole experience comes back to me after the lapse of forty and more years—the soothing rustle of the waves, and the saline smell—boyhood's times, the clam-digging, barefoot, and with trousers roll'd up—hauling down the creek—the perfume of the sedge meadows—the hay-boat, and the chowder and fishing excursions.

Focused and transformed into a great poem, Whitman's description of the formative influence of the seashore becomes "Out of the Cradle Endlessly Rocking," included here in its entirety. In it Whitman unfolds a kind of poetry not possible in shorter lyrics. Besides describing the origin of his vocation as a poet, it demonstrates how Whitman was shaped by nature and by other influences as well. Whitman loved nature from his earliest days. Later he developed a passion for opera. What does it sound like when the natural world and opera come together? The answer is "Out of the Cradle," which Whitman said had to be read aloud to be understood.

"Out of the Cradle" addresses not only personal origins, but also death. At the end of the poem, in one of his most memorable passages, he hears death whispered in the water, hissing into the sand, and he calls it "the low and delicious word…, rustling at my feet, … laving me softly all over." D. H. Lawrence, one of Whitman's most caustic critics and eloquent advocates in one skin, thought he went too far in his attitude toward death—too much merging and union for the high-strung and combative Lawrence. Some psychological critics have suggested that there is something pathological in Whitman's attitude toward death, and it is true that a statement like "to die is different from what any one supposed, and luckier," or a phrase like "whispers of heavenly death," or a poem like "A Clear Midnight"—

Earth, My Likeness

This is thy hour O soul, thy free flight into the wordless,
Away from books, away from art, the day erased, the lesson done,
Thee fully forth emerging, silent, gazing, pondering the themes thou lovest best,
Night, sleep, death and the stars.

—can make Whitman seem a little too friendly with death.

But Whitman's attitude toward death is really not morbid. Rather, it is common sense raised to the level of poetry and wisdom. He was fully aware of the loss that is in death, and felt it keenly. He grieved for dying and dead soldiers. He was hit hard by the death of his mother. Before her funeral, he sat for hours beside the casket in silence, now and then thumping the floor hard with his cane. In "This Compost" he says he is "terrified at the Earth, it is that calm and patient," as it accepts the leavings of death. But for all that, there is in his poetry a pervasive realization that death is simply part of the earth's way of doing business. He knows that it is only with an awareness of the fact of death that we see life truly. Whatever else death is, it is part of nature:

And as to you Corpse I think you are good manure, but that does not offend me,
I smell the white roses sweet-scented and growing,
I reach to the leafy lips, I reach to the polish'd breasts of melons.

It is an ending in one way, and a change in another:

And as to you Life I reckon you are the leavings of many deaths,
(No doubt I have died myself ten thousand times before.)

In death there is both grief and release:

Beautiful that war and all its deeds of carnage must in time be utterly lost,
That the hands of the sisters Death and Night incessantly softly wash again, and
ever again, this soil'd world....

He sensed something immortal in it: "The smallest sprout shows there is really no death." At one time he says, "I cannot answer the question of appearances or that of identity beyond the grave"; at other times, he seems as sure about the individual soul's survival as a priest or minister at a funeral.

We disappear into the earth. It's a mystery. It's all right; don't panic, Whitman seems to say. There are many striking passages in Whitman's poetry about death, but if we had to choose one that gets to the heart of the matter, it might be these lines with which he concludes his greatest poem, "Song of Myself":

I bequeath myself to the dirt to grow from the grass I love,
If you want me again look for me under your boot-soles.

Not all of Whitman's nature poetry is in his poems. If we're open to a definition of poetry that includes prose—prose-poems, poetic prose—then there is a lot of poetry in Whitman's collection *Specimen Days*. Whether one wants to call it poetry or not, most of the best nature writing of Whitman's later life is in this book. Whitman's poetry tended to become more abstract and formal in its diction as he got older. In his later poems, we don't find startlingly specific images as frequently as in the earlier work, and he began to employ "thee" and "thou" as much as any nineteenth-century poet. But in his prose, his sharpness of observation, casual tone, and tangy phrasing stayed with him. (He maintained those qualities in his conversation as well, as is clear in the comments recorded in the final years of his life by his friend Horace Traubel, edited by Gary Schmidgall as *Intimate with Walt*.) *Specimen Days* is very much a miscellany— "incongruous and full of skips and jumps," as Whitman says. He was fully aware of its randomness and roughness: "May-be, if I don't do anything else, I shall send out the most wayward, spontaneous and fragmentary book ever printed." It worked, and in this case a spontaneous and fragmentary approach produced many passages that feel like poetry. They are a relaxed, here-and-now sort of poems. A more elaborate composition such as "Out of the Cradle" is magnificent, and it is clearly an artistic performance, like opera. The prose excursions and observations of *Specimen Days* are casual, more like walks in the woods or letters from a friend.

Certain passages in *Specimen Days* give us our clearest sense that for Whitman nature was not only beautiful and mysterious but therapeutic as well. They were written when he was recovering from a series of strokes—brought on, he thought, as a result of his work in the war hospitals—which had left him partly paralyzed. At about the same time, there was the death of his mother, "the saddest loss and sorrow of my life," and that of a sister-in-law for whom he felt a special fondness, who died young and painfully from cancer or tuberculosis. Whitman was at a low ebb, living mostly confined indoors at his brother's home in Camden, New Jersey. Relief and recovery came at a place twelve miles out in the country, Timber Creek (now Laurel Springs), where he found new friends and could again immerse himself in the natural world. In the woods along the creek he gave himself physical and spiritual therapy—taking sunbaths and mud baths, strolling nude, wrestling with saplings, singing. He spoke of "the natural-medicinal, elemental-moral influences of the spot." He said that they may have saved his life.

Not all of *Specimen Days* is nature writing. It also includes reminiscences from early life, Civil War journals, reflections on literature, and more. But in the middle of the book, after giving a list of wildflowers he's observed, Whitman inserts this:

A CIVILITY TOO LONG NEGLECTED

The forgoing reminds me of something. As the individualities I would mainly portray have certainly been slighted by folks who make pictures, volumes, poems, out of them—as faint testimonial of my own gratitude for many hours of peace and comfort in half-sickness, (and not by any means sure but they will somehow get wind of the compliment,) I hereby dedicate the last half of these SPECIMEN DAYS to the

bees,

black-birds,

dragon-flies,

pond-turtles,

mulleins, tansy, peppermint,

moths (great and little, some
   splendid fellows,)

glow-worms, (swarming millions
   of them indescribably strange and
   beautiful at night over the pond
   and creek,)

water-snakes,

crows,

millers,

mosquitoes,

butterflies,

wasps and hornets,

cat-birds (and all other birds,)

cedars,

tulip-trees (and all other trees,)

and to the spots and memories
   of those days, and of the creek.

Generally Whitman liked more space to work in than Basho and Issa, but he was their brother nonetheless in specificity, and in his affection for ordinary creatures, right down to the insects. There's a mixture of playfulness and reverence in him, and I think sometimes readers get the reverence but miss the playfulness.

Whitman's gesture of "civility" makes a beautiful dedication, and it would serve for this book as well as for *Specimen Days*.

※ ※ ※

"Earth, my likeness" is a striking phrase. It seemed to me the right title for a selection of Whitman's nature writing, yet it does raise the question of just what Whitman had in mind when he compared himself to the earth. Isn't that a pretty far-fetched comparison? The earth itself—rivers, oceans, mountains, forests, swamps, plains, deserts; the turning globe; implacable, inscrutable nature—where does Whitman get off claiming a resemblance to the earth? How accurate can the comparison be? Well, Whitman was audacious, and he enjoyed making large claims. In fact, comparing himself to the earth wasn't enough; he referred to himself as "a kosmos" as well.

The poem "Earth, My Likeness" comes from the "Calamus" group, Whitman's celebration of love between men. In that poem he senses in the earth "something fierce" that might "burst forth." He says that he and an athlete are in love with each other and that some comparable force might burst forth between them. That is the point of comparison in that particular poem. This leads to another question—one that has been the subject of much debate: other than poems, just what forms of expression did Whitman's affection and desire take? Gary Schmidgall's *Walt Whitman: A Gay Life* is one book that argues for Whitman's active homosexuality, and Jonathan Ned Katz's *Love Stories: Sex between Men before Homosexuality* presents a fascinating and nuanced examination of the subject.

That Whitman was gay in his feelings is pretty clear, though over the years many have denied or recast even that. We know that he wrote about men and his attraction to them a whole lot more, and a whole lot more urgently, than he did about women. We know he enjoyed putting his arm over a buddy's shoulders, and that he kissed men feelingly and slept with them. But in the nineteenth century same-sex shows of affection and sleeping together were more commonplace, right? Did the penis—"this poem drooping shy and unseen that I always carry, and that all men carry,...our lusty lurking masculine poems"—get involved? Besides the poems, Whitman left many clues and counter-clues about his love life, but we don't know the answer to that question for sure. Maybe that was the desire "eligible to burst forth" that he was feeling when he wrote "Earth, My Likeness."

However that may be, we have other testimony than Whitman's own that he did in fact resemble the earth. It comes from John Burroughs, who was Whitman's friend and who became one of the best-known nature essayists of his time. He had been reading Whitman's poetry, and then met the man himself. Here is his description of their first meeting:

> His book, read with modern eyes, would seem to justify Emerson's characterization of him as "half song thrush and half alligator;" and, by some means or other, I had got an impression that he was at least half-rowdy. Imagine my surprise, therefore, when I beheld a well-dressed, large, benevolent-looking man, cleanly and neat, with a grizzly, shaggy appearance about the face and open throat.
>
> Without rising he reached out to me a large, warm, soft hand, and regarded me with a look of infinite good nature and contentment. I was struck with the strange new beauty of him as he sat there in the gaslight—the brightness of his eyes, the glow of his countenance, and the curious blending of youth and age in his expression. He was in that felicitous mood almost habitual to him, I have since found, during which his flesh and skin become, as it were, transparent, and allow his great summery, motherly soul to shine through.

Burroughs also wrote:

Notwithstanding the beauty and expressiveness of his eyes, I occasionally see something in them as he bends them upon me, that almost makes me draw back. I cannot explain it—whether it is more, or less, than human. It is as if the earth looked at me—dumb, yearning, immodest, inhuman [unhuman?]. If the impersonal elements and forces were concentrated in an eye, that would be it.

In a letter to a friend, Burroughs said:

I have been much with Walt. Have even slept with him. I love him very much. The more I see and talk with him, the greater he becomes to me. He is as vast as the earth, and as loving and noble.

And three weeks later:

The more I see of Walt, the more I like him.... He is far the wisest man I have ever met. There is nothing more to be said after he gives his views; it is as if Nature herself had spoken.

Burroughs was heterosexual—you might say a flaming heterosexual (though *heterosexual,* like *homosexual,* is our term, not the nineteenth century's). His marriage was unhappy because of his wife's unresponsiveness to his sexual advances; he fathered his son with a local girl; the great love of his life was a woman he met when he was sixty-four and she was thirty-three. I won't try to unravel whatever sexual undercurrents there may be in Burroughs's feelings about Whitman; in fact, I'd rather leave them raveled. Sexuality is a great, flowing force. We don't have it so much as it has us. In that way it is like the earth, and the instinctual life that we share with the other animals. Maybe what Burroughs was trying to say when he reached for earth images in describing what he felt in and for Whitman was this: he had met someone who seemed to him a force of nature.

Thinking back at the end of his life to Emerson's attempt to persuade him to take some of the sex out of *Leaves of Grass*, Whitman said, "If I had cut sex out I might just as well have cut everything out." The sex in his poetry is not located in just a few poems; it suffuses much more than an erotic or taboo poem here and there. When Whitman wrote about sex, he often wrote about it in terms of the natural world, and when he wrote about the natural world, he often wrote about it in terms of sexual intimacy and pleasure. The poems "Spontaneous Me" and "These I Singing in Spring" are perhaps the premier examples; no other walks in the woods in literature are quite like them. Eros and nature are richly tangled in a wet, lush bouquet, and Whitman does not want us to separate them. The Jesuit poet Gerard Manley Hopkins probably comes closest to this effect, though his idea was that it is Christ and nature that are entangled. Hopkins said about Whitman, "I always knew in my heart Walt Whitman's mind to be more like my own than any other man's living. As he is a great scoundrel this is not a pleasant confession." Hopkins too recognized something wild, elemental, and pre-Christian in Whitman.

Whitman was a grateful guest of the earth. He was a model in that respect: out of gratitude for the pleasure of being alive on the earth, he became one of the great praisers. He liked to be outdoors. He did much of his reading and writing there. He was a walker. He liked to recite poetry in the open air. He liked to loaf; his most famous description of a mystical experience begins, "Loafe with me on the grass...." He had enormous capacity for enjoyment and amazement—sometimes in calm observation; sometimes as exuberance; sometimes as ecstasy. (And sometimes, besides these feelings and states of consciousness, there was despair as well.) Writing about sex as nature and nature as sex is more than a strategy or technique for Whitman. It is a measure of his happiness in being open to and in touch with the ground, the green world, animals, the water, the air, and the stars. His simple and brilliant title, *Leaves of Grass*, was just right for a book that grew so much out of the earth.

TWO POEMS

There Was a Child Went Forth

There was a child went forth every day,
And the first object he look'd upon, that object he became,
And that object became part of him for the day or a certain part of the day,
Or for many years or stretching cycles of years.

The early lilacs became part of this child,
And grass and white and red morning-glories, and white and red clover,
    and the song of the phoebe-bird,
And the Third-month lambs and the sow's pink-faint litter, and the mare's
    foal and the cow's calf,
And the noisy brood of the barnyard or by the mire of the pond-side,
And the fish suspending themselves so curiously below there, and the
    beautiful curious liquid,
And the water-plants with their graceful flat heads, all became part of him.

The field-sprouts of Fourth-month and Fifth-month became part of him,
Winter-grain sprouts and those of the light-yellow corn, and the esculent
    roots of the garden,
And the apple-trees cover'd with blossoms and the fruit afterward, and
    wood-berries, and the commonest weeds by the road,
And the old drunkard staggering home from the outhouse of the tavern
    whence he had lately risen,
And the schoolmistress that pass'd on her way to the school,
And the friendly boys that pass'd, and the quarrelsome boys,
And the tidy and fresh-cheek'd girls, and the barefoot negro boy and girl,
And all the changes of city and country wherever he went.

His own parents, he that had father'd him and she that had conceiv'd
    him in her womb and birth'd him,
They gave this child more of themselves than that,
They gave him afterward every day, they became part of him.

The mother at home quietly placing the dishes on the supper-table,
The mother with mild words, clean her cap and gown, a wholesome
    odor falling off her person and clothes as she walks by,
The father, strong, self-sufficient, manly, mean, anger'd, unjust,

The blow, the quick loud word, the tight bargain, the crafty lure,

The family usages, the language, the company, the furniture, the yearning and swelling heart,

Affection that will not be gainsay'd, the sense of what is real, the thought if after all it should prove unreal,

The doubts of day-time and the doubts of night-time, the curious whether and how,

Whether that which appears so is so, or is it all flashes and specks?

Men and women crowding fast in the streets, if they are not flashes and specks what are they?

The streets themselves and the facades of houses, and goods in the windows,

Vehicles, teams, the heavy-plank'd wharves, the huge crossing at the ferries,

The village on the highland seen from afar at sunset, the river between,

Shadows, aureola and mist, the light falling on roofs and gables of white or brown two miles off,

The schooner near by sleepily dropping down the tide, the little boat slack-tow'd astern,

The hurrying tumbling waves, quick-broken crests, slapping,

The strata of color'd clouds, the long bar of maroon-tint away solitary by itself, the spread of purity it lies motionless in,

The horizon's edge, the flying sea-crow, the fragrance of salt marsh and shore mud,

These became part of that child who went forth every day, and who now goes, and will always go forth every day.

This Compost

1

Something startles me where I thought I was safest,
I withdraw from the still woods I loved,
I will not go now on the pastures to walk,
I will not strip the clothes from my body to meet my lover the sea,
I will not touch my flesh to the earth as to other flesh to renew me.

O how can it be that the ground itself does not sicken?
How can you be alive you growths of spring?
How can you furnish health you blood of herbs, roots, orchards, grain?
Are they not continually putting distemper'd corpses within you?
Is not every continent worked over and over with sour dead?

Where have you disposed of their carcasses?
Those drunkards and gluttons of so many generations?
Where have you drawn off all the foul liquid and meat?
I do not see any of it upon you to-day, or perhaps I am deceived,
I will run a furrow with my plough, I will press my spade through
　　the sod and turn it up underneath,
I am sure I shall expose some of the foul meat.

2

Behold this compost! behold it well!
Perhaps every mite has once form'd part of a sick person—yet behold!
The grass of spring covers the prairies,
The bean bursts noiselessly through the mould in the garden,
The delicate spear of the onion pierces upward,

The apple-buds cluster together on the apple-branches,

The resurrection of the wheat appears with pale visage out of its graves,

The tinge awakes over the willow-tree and the mulberry-tree,

The he-birds carol mornings and evenings while the she-birds sit on
their nests,

The young of poultry break through the hatch'd eggs,

The new-born of animals appear, the calf is dropt from the cow, the colt
from the mare,

Out of its little hill faithfully rise the potato's dark green leaves,

Out of its hill rises the yellow maize-stalk, the lilacs bloom in the
dooryards,

The summer growth is innocent and disdainful above all those strata
of sour dead.

What chemistry!

That the winds are really not infectious,

That this is no cheat, this transparent green-wash of the sea which is so
amorous after me,

That it is safe to allow it to lick my naked body all over with its tongues,

That it will not endanger me with the fevers that have deposited
themselves in it.

That all is clean forever and forever,

That the cool drink from the well tastes so good,

That blackberries are so flavorous and juicy,

That the fruits of the apple-orchard and the orange-orchard, that melons,
grapes, peaches, plums, will none of them poison me,

That when I recline on the grass I do not catch any disease,

Though probably every spear of grass rises out of what was once a
catching disease.

Earth, My Likeness

Now I am terrified at the Earth, it is that calm and patient,
It grows such sweet things out of such corruptions,
It turns harmless and stainless on its axis, with such
    endless successions of diseas'd corpses,
It distills such exquisite winds out of such infused fetor,
It renews with such unwitting looks its prodigal, annual,
    sumptuous crops,
It gives such divine materials to men, and accepts such
    leavings from them at last.

EARTHLY PLEASURES,
FEELING ALIVE

from Song of Myself

The atmosphere is not a perfume, it has no taste of the distillation,
    it is odorless,
It is for my mouth forever, I am in love with it,
I will go to the bank by the wood and become undisguised and naked,
I am mad for it to be in contact with me.
The smoke of my own breath,
Echoes, ripples, buzz'd whispers, love-root, silk-thread, crotch and vine,
My respiration and inspiration, the beating of my heart, the passing of
    blood and air through my lungs,
The sniff of green leaves and dry leaves, and of the shore and dark-
    color'd sea-rocks, and of hay in the barn,
The sound of the belch'd words of my voice loos'd to the eddies
    of the wind,
A few light kisses, a few embraces, a reaching around of arms,
The play of shine and shade on the trees as the supple boughs wag,
The delight alone or in the rush of the streets, or along the fields
    and hill-sides,
The feeling of health, the full-noon trill, the song of me rising from bed
    and meeting the sun.

from Song of Myself

I am he that walks with the tender and growing night,
I call to the earth and sea half-held by the night.

Press close bare-bosom'd night—press close magnetic nourishing night!
Night of south winds—night of the large few stars!
Still nodding night—mad naked summer night.

Smile O voluptuous cool-breath'd earth!
Earth of the slumbering and liquid trees!
Earth of departed sunset—earth of the mountains misty-topt!
Earth of the vitreous pour of the full moon just tinged with blue!
Earth of shine and dark mottling the tide of the river!
Earth of the limpid gray of clouds brighter and clearer for my sake!
Far-swooping elbow'd earth—rich apple-blossom'd earth!
Smile, for your lover comes.

Earth, My Likeness

from Song of Myself

Divine am I inside and out, and I make holy whatever I touch or
    am touch'd from,
The scent of these arm-pits aroma finer than prayer,
This head more than churches, bibles, and all the creeds.

If I worship one thing more than another it shall be the spread
    of my own body, or any part of it,
Translucent mould of me it shall be you!
Shaded ledges and rests it shall be you!
Firm masculine colter it shall be you!
Whatever goes to the tilth of me it shall be you!
You my rich blood! your milky stream pale strippings of my life!
Breast that presses against other breasts it shall be you!
My brain it shall be your occult convolutions!
Root of wash'd sweet-flag! timorous pond-snipe! nest of guarded
    duplicate eggs! it shall be you!
Mix'd tussled hay of head, beard, brawn, it shall be you!
Trickling sap of maple, fibre of manly wheat, it shall be you!
Sun so generous it shall be you!
Vapors lighting and shading my face it shall be you!
You sweaty brooks and dews it shall be you!
Winds whose soft-tickling genitals rub against me it shall be you!
Broad muscular fields, branches of live oak, loving lounger in my
    winding paths, it shall be you!
Hands I have taken, face I have kiss'd, mortal I have ever touch'd,
    it shall be you.

Me Imperturbe

Me imperturbe, standing at ease in Nature,

Master of all or mistress of all, aplomb in the midst of irrational things,

Imbued as they, passive, receptive, silent as they,

Finding my occupation, poverty, notoriety, foibles, crimes, less
    important than I thought,

Me toward the Mexican sea, or in the Mannahatta or the Tennessee, or
    far north or inland,

A river man, or a man of the woods, or of any farm-life of these States
    or of the coast, or the lakes or Kanada,

Me wherever my life is lived, O to be self-balanced for contingencies,

To confront night, storms, hunger, ridicule, accidents, rebuffs, as the
    trees and animals do.

from Song of Myself

The big doors of the country barn stand open and ready,

The dried grass of the harvest-time loads the slow-drawn wagon,

The clear light plays on the brown gray and green intertinged,

The armfuls are pack'd to the sagging mow.

I am there, I help, I came stretch'd atop the load,

I felt its soft jolts, one leg reclined on the other,

I jump from the cross-beams and seize the clover and timothy,

And roll head over heels and tangle my hair full of wisps.

from A Song of Joys

O boating on the rivers,
The voyage down the St. Lawrence, the superb scenery, the steamers,
The ships sailing, the Thousand Islands, the occasional timber-raft
    and the raftsmen with long-reaching sweep-oars,
The little huts on the rafts, and the steam of smoke when they cook
    supper at evening.

Earth, My Likeness

from Song of Myself

Upon a door-step, upon the horse-block of hard wood outside,
Upon the race-course, or enjoying picnics or jigs on a good game of baseball,
At he-festivals, with blackguard gibes, ironical license, bull-dances, drinking, laughter,
At the cider-mill tasting the sweets of the brown mash, sucking the juice through
    a straw,
At apple-peelings wanting kisses for all the red fruit I find,
At musters, beach-parties, friendly bees, huskings, house-raisings;
Where the mocking-bird sounds his delicious gurgles, cackles, screams, weeps,
Where the hay-rick stands in the barn-yard, where the dry-stalks are scatter'd,
    where the brood-cow waits in the hovel,
Where the bull advances to do his masculine work, where the stud to the mare,
    where the cock is treading the hen,
Where the heifers browse, where geese nip their food with short jerks,
Where the sun-down shadows lengthen over the limitless and lonesome prairie,
Where herds of buffalo make a crawling spread of the square miles far and near,
Where the humming-bird shimmers, where the neck of the long-lived swan is curving
    and winding,
Where the laughing-gull scoots by the shore, where she laughs her near-human laugh,
Where bee hives range on a gray bench in the garden half hid by the high weeds,
Where band-neck'd partridges roost in a ring on the ground with their heads out,
Where burial coaches enter the arch'd gates of a cemetery,
Where winter wolves bark amid wastes of snow and icicled trees,
Where the yellow-crown'd heron comes to the edge of the marsh at night
    and feeds upon small crabs,
Where the splash of swimmers and divers cools the warm noon,
Where the katy-did works her chromatic reed on the walnut-tree
    over the well...

Earthly Pleasures, Feeling Alive

To the Spring and Brook

So, still sauntering on, to the spring under the willows—musical as soft clinking glasses—pouring a sizeable stream, thick as my neck, pure and clear, out from its vent where the bank arches over like a great brown shaggy eyebrow or mouth-roof—gurgling, gurgling ceaselessly—meaning, saying something, of course (if one could only translate it)—always gurgling there, the whole year through—never giving out—oceans of mint, blackberries in summer— choice of light and shade—just the place for my July sun-baths and water-baths too—but mainly the inimitable soft sound-gurgles of it, as I sit there hot afternoons. How they and all grow into me, day after day—everything in keeping—the wild, just-palpable perfume, and the dapple of leaf-shadows, and all the natural-medicinal, elemental-moral influences of the spot.

Earth, My Likeness

A Sun-Bath—Nakedness

Sunday, Aug. 27.—An hour or so after breakfast I wended my way down to the recesses of the aforesaid dell, which I and certain thrushes, cat-birds, &c., had all to ourselves. A light south-west wind was blowing through the tree-tops. It was just the place and time for my Adamic air-bath and flesh-brushing from head to foot. So hanging clothes on a rail near by, keeping old broadbrim straw on head and easy shoes on feet, haven't I had a good time the last two hours! First with the stiff elastic bristles rasping arms, breast, sides, till they turn'd scarlet—then partially bathing in the clear waters of the running brook—taking everything very leisurely, with many rests and pauses—stepping about barefooted every few minutes now and then in some neighboring black ooze, for unctuous mud-bath to my feet—a brief second and third rinsing in the crystal running waters—rubbing with the fragrant towel—slow negligent promenades on the turf up and down in the sun, varied with occasional rests, and further frictions of the bristle-brush—sometimes carrying my portable chair with me from place to place, as my range is quite extensive here, nearly a hundred rods, feeling quite secure from intrusion, (and that indeed I am not at all nervous about, if it accidentally happens.)

As I walk'd slowly over the grass, the sun shone out enough to show the shadow moving with me. Somehow I seem'd to get identity with each and every thing around me, in its condition. Nature was naked, and I was also.

Happiness and Raspberries

June 21.—Here I am, on the west bank of the Hudson, 80 miles north of New York, near Esopus, at the handsome, roomy, honeysuckle-and-rose-embower'd cottage of John Burroughs. The place, the perfect June days and nights, (leaning toward crisp and cool,) the hospitality of J. and Mrs. B., the air, the fruit, (especially my favorite dish, currants and raspberries, mixed, sugar'd, fresh and ripe from the bushes—I pick 'em myself)—the room I occupy at night, the perfect bed, the window giving an ample view of the Hudson and the opposite shores, so wonderful toward sunset, and the rolling music of the RR. trains, far over there—the peaceful rest—the early Venus-heralded dawn—the noiseless splash of sunrise, the light and warmth indescribably glorious, in which, (soon as the sun is well up,) I have a capital rubbing and rasping with the flesh-brush—with an extra scour on the back by Al. J., who is here with us—all inspiriting my invalid frame with new life, for the day. Then, after some whiffs of morning air, the delicious coffee of Mrs. B., with cream, strawberries, and many substantials, for breakfast.

ANIMALS, BIRDS,
and INSECTS

from Song of Myself

I think I could turn and live with animals, they are so placid
   and self-contain'd,
I stand and look at them long and long.

They do not sweat and whine about their condition,
They do not lie awake in the dark and weep for their sins,
They do not make me sick discussing their duty to God,
Not one is dissatisfied, not one is demented with the mania
   of owning things,
Not one kneels to another, nor to his kind that lived thousands
   of years ago,
Not one is respectable or unhappy over the whole earth.

So they show their relations to me and I accept them,
They bring me tokens of myself, they evince them plainly
   in their possession.

I wonder where they get those tokens,
Did I pass that way huge times ago and negligently drop them?

from Starting from Paumanok

As I have walk'd in Alabama my morning walk,
I have seen where the she-bird the mocking-bird sat on her nest
    in the briers hatching her brood.

I have seen the he-bird also,
I have paus'd to hear him near at hand inflating his throat and
    joyfully singing.

And while I paus'd it came to me that what he really sang for
    was not there only,
Nor for his mate nor himself only, nor all sent back by the echoes,
But subtle, clandestine, away beyond,
A charge transmitted and gift occult for those being born.

Earth, My Likeness

The Ox-Tamer

In a far-away northern country in the placid pastoral region,
Lives my farmer friend, the theme of my recitative, a famous tamer of oxen,
There they bring him the three-year-olds and the four-year-olds to break them,
He will take the wildest steer in the world and break him and tame him,
He will go fearless without any whip where the young bullock chafes up and
    down the yard,
The bullock's head tosses restless high in the air with raging eyes,
Yet see you! how soon his rage subsides—how soon this tamer tames him;
See you! on the farms hereabout a hundred oxen young and old, and he
    is the man who has tamed them,
They all know him, all are affectionate to him;
See you! some are such beautiful animals, so lofty looking;
Some are buff-color'd, some mottled, one has a white line running along
    his back, some are brindled,
Some have wide flaring horns (a good sign)—see you the bright hides,
See, the two with stars on their foreheads—see, the round bodies and
    broad backs,
How straight and square they stand on their legs—what fine sagacious eyes!
How they watch their tamer—they wish him near them—how they turn and
    look after him!
What yearning expression! how uneasy they are when he moves away
    from them;
Now I marvel what it can be he appears to them, (books, politics, poems,
    depart—all else departs,)
I confess I envy only his fascination—my silent, illiterate friend,
Whom a hundred oxen love there in his life on farms,
In the northern country far, in the placid pastoral region.

from Song of Myself

In me the caresser of life wherever moving, backward as well as
 forward sluing,
To niches aside and junior bending, not a person or object missing,
Absorbing all to myself and for this song.

Oxen that rattle the yoke and chain or halt in the leafy shade,
 what is that you express in your eyes?
It seems to me more than all the print I have read in my life.

My tread scares the wood-drake and wood-duck on my distant
 and day-long ramble,
They rise together, they slowly circle around.

I believe in those wing'd purposes,
And acknowledge red, yellow, white, playing within me,
And consider green and violet and the tufted crown intentional,
And do not call the tortoise unworthy because she is not
 something else,
And the jay in the woods never studied the gamut, yet trills pretty
 well to me,
And the look of the bay mare shames silliness out of me.

A Meadow Lark

March 16.—Fine, clear, dazzling morning, the sun an hour high, the air just tart enough. What a stamp in advance my whole day receives from the song of that meadow lark perch'd on a fence-stake twenty rods distant! Two or three liquid-simple notes, repeated at intervals, full of careless happiness and hope. With its peculiar shimmering slow progress and rapid-noiseless action of the wings, it flies on a ways, lights on another stake, and so on to another, shimmering and singing many minutes.

from Bumble-Bees

Later.—Nature marches in procession, in sections, like the corps of an army. All have done much for me, and still do. But for the last two days it has been the great wild bee, the humble-bee, or "bumble," as the children call him. As I walk, or hobble, from the farm-house down to the creek, I traverse the before-mention'd lane, fenced by old rails, with many splits, splinters, breaks, holes, &c., the choice habitat of those crooning, hairy insects. Up and down and by and between these rails, they swarm and dart and fly in countless myriads. As I wend slowly along, I am often accompanied with a moving cloud of them. They play a leading part in my morning, midday or sun-set rambles, and often dominate the landscape in a way I never before thought of—fill the long lane, not by scores or hundreds only, but by thousands. Large and vivacious and swift, with wonderful momentum and a loud swelling perpetual hum, varied now and then with something almost like a shriek, they dart to and fro, in rapid flashes, chasing each other, and (little things as they are,) conveying to me a new and pronounc'd sense of strength, beauty, vitality and movement. Are they in their mating season? or what is the meaning of this plenitude, swiftness, eagerness, display? As I walk'd, I thought I was followed by a particular swarm, but upon observation I saw that it was a rapid succession of changing swarms, one after another.

As I write, I am seated under a big wild-cherry tree—the warm day temper'd by partial clouds and a fresh breeze, neither too heavy nor light—and here I sit long and long, envelop'd in the deep musical drone of these bees, flitting, balancing, darting to and fro about me by hundreds—big fellows with light yellow jackets, great glistening swelling bodies, stumpy heads and gauzy wings—humming their perpetual rich mellow boom. (Is there not a hint in it for a musical composition, of which it should be the back-ground? some bumble-bee symphony?) How it all nourishes, lulls me, in the way most needed; the open air, the rye-fields, the apple orchards. The last two days have been faultless in sun, breeze, temperature and everything; never two more perfect days, and I have enjoy'd them wonderfully. My health is somewhat better, and my spirit at peace. (Yet the anniversary of the saddest loss and sorrow of my life is close at hand.)

Another jotting, another perfect day: forenoon, from 7 to 9, two hours envelop'd in sound of bumble-bees and bird-music. Down in the apple-trees and in a neighboring cedar were three or four russet-back'd thrushes, each singing his best; and roulading in ways I never heard surpass'd. Two hours I abandon myself to hearing them, and indolently absorbing the scene. Almost every bird I notice has a special time in the year—sometimes limited to a few days—when it sings its best; and now is the period of these russet-backs. Meanwhile, up and down the lane, the darting, droning, musical bumble-bees. A great swarm again for my entourage as I return home, moving along with me as before.

Sundown Perfume—Quail-Notes —The Hermit Thrush

June 19th, 4 to 6 1/2 P.M.—Sitting alone by the creek—solitude here, but the scene bright and vivid enough—the sun shining, and quite a fresh wind blowing (some heavy showers last night,) the grass and trees looking their best—the clare-obscure of different greens, shadows, half-shadows, and the dappling glimpses of water, through recesses—the wild flageolet-note of a quail nearby—the just-heard fretting of some hylas down there in the pond—crows cawing in the distance—a drove of young hogs rooting in soft ground near the oak near which I sit—some come sniffing near me, and then scamper away with grunts. And still the clear notes of the quail—the quiver of leave-shadows over the paper as I write—the sky aloft, with white clouds, and the sun well declining to the west—the swift darting of many sand-swallows coming and going, their holes in a neighboring marl-bank—the odor of the cedar and oak, so palpable, as evening approaches—perfume, color, the bronze-and-gold of nearly ripen'd wheat—clover-fields, with honey-scent—the well-up maize, with long and rustling leaves—the great patches of thriving potatoes, dusky green, fleck'd all over with white blossoms—the old, warty, venerable oak above me—and ever, mix'd with the dual tones of the quail, the soughing of the wind through some near-by pines.

As I rise for return, I linger long to a delicious song-epilogue (is it the hermit-thrush?) from some bushy recess off there in the swamp, repeated leisurely and pensively over and over again. This, to the circle-gambols of the swallows flying by dozens in concentric rings in the last rays of sunset, like flashes of some airy wheel.

from Hudson River Sights

But there is one sight the very grandest. Sometimes in the fiercest driving storm of wind, rain, hail or snow, a great eagle will appear over the river, now soaring with steady and now overhended wings—always confronting the gale, or perhaps cleaving into, or at times literally *sitting* upon it. It is like reading some first-class natural tragedy or epic, or hearing martial trumpets. The splendid bird enjoys the hubbub—is adjusted and equal to it—finishes it so artistically. His pinions just oscillating—the position of his head and neck—his resistless, occasionally varied flight—now a swirl, now an upward movement—the black clouds driving—the angry wash below—the hiss of rain, the wind's piping (perhaps the ice colliding, grunting)—he tacking or jibing—now, as it were, for a change, abandoning himself to the gale, moving with it with such velocity—and now, resuming control, he comes up against it, lord of the situation and the storm—lord, amid it, of power and savage joy.

The Dalliance of the Eagles

Skirting the river road, (my forenoon walk, my rest,)
Skyward in air a sudden muffled sound, the dalliance of the eagles,
The rushing amorous contact high in space together,
The clinching interlocking claws, a living, fierce, gyrating wheel,
Four beating wings, two beaks, a swirling mass tight grappling,
In tumbling turning clustering loops, straight downward falling,
Till o'er the river pois'd, the twain yet one, a moment's lull,
A motionless still balance in the air, then parting, talons loosing,
Upward again on slow-firm pinions slanting, their separate diverse flight,
She hers, he his, pursuing.

An Unknown

June 15.—To-day I noticed a new large bird, size of a nearly grown hen—a haughty, white-bodied dark-wing'd hawk—I suppose a hawk from his bill and general look—only he had a clear, loud, quite musical, sort of bell-like call, which he repeated again and again, at intervals, from a lofty dead tree-top, over-hanging the water. Sat there a long time, and I on the opposite bank watching him. Then he darted down, skimming pretty close to the stream—rose slowly, a magnificent sight, and sail'd with steady wide-spread wings, no flapping at all, up and down the pond two or three times, near me, in circles in clear sight, as if for my delectation. Once he came quite close over my head; I saw plainly his hook'd bill and hard restless eyes.

Crows and Crows

Nov. 14.—As I sit here by the creek, resting after my walk, a warm languor bathes me from the sun. No sound but a cawing of crows, and no motion but their black flying figures from overhead, reflected in the mirror of the pond below. Indeed a principal feature of the scene to-day is these crows, their incessant cawing, far or near, and their countless flocks and processions moving from place to place, and at times almost darkening the air with their myriads. As I sit a moment writing this by the bank, I see the black, clear-cut reflection of them far below, flying through the watery looking-glass, by ones, twos, or long strings. All last night I heard the noises from their great roost in a neighboring wood.

Animals, Birds, and Insects

Locusts and Katydids

Aug. 22.—Reedy monotones of locusts, or sounds of katydid—I hear the latter at night, and the other both day and night. I thought the morning and evening warble of birds delightful; but I find I can listen to these strange insects with just as much pleasure. A single locust is now heard near noon from a tree two hundred feet off, as I write—a long, whirring, continued, quite loud noise graded in distinct whirls, or swinging circles, increasing in strength and rapidity up to a certain point, and then a fluttering, quietly tapering fall. Each strain is continued from one to two minutes. The locust-song is very appropriate to the scene—gushes, has meaning, is masculine, is like some fine old wine, not sweet, but far better than sweet.

But the katydid—how shall I describe its piquant utterances? One sings from a willow-tree just outside my open bedroom window, twenty yards distant; every clear night for a fortnight past has sooth'd me to sleep. I rode through

a piece of woods for a hundred rods the other evening, and heard the katydids by myriads—very curious for once; but I like better my single neighbor on the tree.

from Song of Myself

A gigantic beauty of a stallion, fresh and responsive to my caresses,
Head high in the forehead, wide between the ears,
Limbs glossy and supple, tail dusting the ground,
Eyes full of sparkling wickedness, ears finely cut, flexibly moving.

His nostrils dilate as my heels embrace him,
His well-built limbs tremble with pleasure as we race around and return.

I but use you a minute, then I resign you, stallion,
Why do I need your paces when I myself out-gallop them?
Even as I stand or sit passing faster than you.

A Noiseless Patient Spider

A noiseless patient spider,
I mark'd where on a little promontory it stood isolated,
Mark'd how to explore the vacant vast surrounding,
It launch'd forth filament, filament, filament, out of itself,
Ever unreeling them, ever tirelessly speeding them.

And you O my soul where you stand,
Surrounded, detached, in measureless oceans of space,
Ceaselessly musing, venturing, throwing, seeking the spheres to
    connect them,
Till the bridge you will need be form'd, till the ductile anchor hold,
Till the gossamer thread you fling catch somewhere, O my soul.

Miracles

Why, who makes much of a miracle?
As to me I know of nothing else but miracles,
Whether I walk the streets of Manhattan,
Or dart my sight over the roofs of houses toward the sky,
Or wade with naked feet along the beach just in the edge of the water,
Or stand under trees in the woods,
Or talk by day with any one I love, or sleep in the bed at night with any one
     I love,
Or sit at table at dinner with the rest,
Or look at strangers opposite me riding in the car,
Or watch honey-bees busy around the hive of a summer forenoon,
Or animals feeding in the fields,
Or birds, or the wonderfulness of insects in the air,
Or the wonderfulness of the sundown, or of stars shining so quiet and bright,
Or the exquisite delicate thin curve of the new moon in spring,
These with the rest, one and all, are to me miracles,
The whole referring, yet each distinct and in its place.

To me every hour of the light and dark is a miracle,
Every cubic inch of space is a miracle,
Every square yard of the surface of the earth is spread with the same,
Every foot of the interior swarms with the same.

To me the sea is a continual miracle,
The fishes that swim—the rocks—the motion of the waves—the ships
     with men in them,
What stranger miracles are there?

from Song of Myself

I believe a leaf of grass is no less than the journey-work of the stars,
And the pismire is equally perfect, and a grain of sand, and the egg
   of the wren,
And the tree-toad is a chef-d'oeuvre for the highest,
And the running blackberry would adorn the parlors of heaven,
And the narrowest hinge in my hand puts to scorn all machinery,
And the cow crunching with depress'd head surpasses any statue,
And a mouse is miracle enough to stagger sextillions of infidels.

Until You Can Explain

Priests!
Until you can explain a paving stone, do not try to explain God:
Until your creeds can do as much as apples and hen's eggs,
   let down your eyebrows a little,
Until your Bibles and prayer-books are able to walk like me,
And until your brick and mortar can procreate as I can,
I beg you, Sirs, do not presume to put them above me.

Orange Buds by Mail from Florida

[Voltaire closed a famous argument by claiming that a ship of war and the grand opera were proofs enough of civilization's and France's progress, in his day.]

A lesser proof than old Voltaire's, yet greater,

Proof of this present time, and thee, thy broad expanse, America,

To my plain Northern hut, in outside clouds and snow,

Brought safely for a thousand miles o'er land and tide,

Some three days since on their own soil live-sprouting,

Now here their sweetness through my room unfolding,

A bunch of orange buds by mail from Florida.

Thoughts under an Oak—A Dream

June 2.—This is the fourth day of a dark northeast storm, wind and rain. Day before yesterday was my birthday. I have now enter'd on my 60th year. Every day of the storm, protected by overshoes and a waterproof blanket, I regularly come down to the pond, and ensconce myself under the lee of the great oak; I am here now writing these lines. The dark smoke-color'd clouds roll in furious silence athwart the sky; the soft green leaves dangle all round me; the wind steadily keeps up its hoarse, soothing music over my head—Nature's mighty whisper. Seated here in solitude I have been musing over my life—connecting events, dates, as links of a chain, neither sadly nor cheerily, but somehow, to-day here under the oak, in the rain, in an unusually matter-of-fact spirit.

But my great oak—sturdy, vital, green—five feet thick at the butt. I sit a great deal near or under him. Then the tulip tree near by—the Apollo of the woods—tall and graceful, yet robust and sinewy, inimitable in hang of foliage and throwing-out of limb; as if the beauteous, vital, leafy creature could walk, if it only would. (I had a sort of dream-trance the other day, in which I saw my favorite trees step out and promenade up, down and around, very curiously—with a whisper from one, leaning down as he pass'd me, *We do all this on the present occasion, exceptionally, just for you.*)

from The Lesson of a Tree

Sept. 1.—I should not take either the biggest or the most picturesque tree to illustrate it. Here is one of my favorites now before me, a fine yellow poplar, quite straight, perhaps 90 feet high, and four thick at the butt. How strong, vital, enduring! how dumbly eloquent! What suggestions of imperturbability and *being,* as against the human trait of mere *seeming.* Then the qualities, almost emotional, palpably artistic, heroic, of a tree; so innocent and harmless, yet so savage. It *is,* yet says nothing. How it rebukes by its tough and equable serenity all weathers, this gusty-temper'd little whiffet, man, that runs indoors at a mite of rain or snow. Science (or rather half-way science) scoffs at reminiscence of dryad and hamadryad, and of trees speaking. But, if they don't, they do as well as most speaking, writing, poetry, sermons—or rather they do a great deal better. I should say indeed that those old dryad-reminiscences are quite as true as any, and profounder than most reminiscences we get. ("Cut this out," as the quack mediciners say, and keep by you.) Go and sit in a grove or woods, with one or more of those voiceless companions, and read the foregoing, and think.

from Debris

I will take an egg out of the robin's nest in the orchard,
I will take a branch of gooseberries from the old bush in the garden,
    and go and preach to the world;
You shall see I will not meet a single heretic or scorner,
You shall see how I stump clergymen, and confound them,
You shall see me showing a scarlet tomato, and a white pebble
    from the beach.

from Song of Myself

A child said What is the grass? fetching it to me with full hands;
How could I answer the child? I do not know what it is any more than he.

I guess it must be the flag of my disposition, out of hopeful green stuff
    woven.

Or I guess it is the handkerchief of the Lord,
A scented gift and remembrancer designedly dropt,
Bearing the owner's name someway in the corners, that we may see and
    remark, and say Whose?

Or I guess the grass is itself a child, the produced babe of the vegetation.

Or I guess it is a uniform hieroglyphic,
And it means, Sprouting alike in broad zones and narrow zones,
Growing among black folks as among white,
Kanuck, Tuckahoe, Congressman, Cuff, I give them the same, I receive
    them the same.

And now it seems to me the beautiful uncut hair of graves.

Tenderly will I use you curling grass,
It may be you transpire from the breasts of young men,
It may be if I had known them I would have loved them,
It may be you are from old people, or from offspring taken soon out of
    their mother's laps,
And here you are the mother's laps.

Earth, My Likeness

This grass is very dark to be from the white heads of old mothers,
Darker than the colorless beards of old men,
Dark to come from under the faint red roofs of mouths.

O I perceive after all so many uttering tongues,
And I perceive they do not come from the roofs of mouths for nothing.

I wish I could translate the hints about the dead young men and women,
And the hints about old men and mothers, and the offspring taken soon out
    of their laps.
What do you think has become of the young and old men?
And what do you think has become of the women and children?

They are alive and well somewhere,
The smallest sprout shows there is really no death,
And if ever there was it led forward life, and does not wait at the end
    to arrest it,
And ceas'd the moment life appear'd.

All goes onward and outward, nothing
    collapses,
And to die is different from what any one
    supposed, and luckier.

from Song of Myself

And as to you Death, and you bitter hug of mortality, it is idle
    to try to alarm me.

To his work without flinching the accoucheur comes,
I see the elder-hand pressing receiving supporting,
I recline by the sills of the exquisite flexible doors,
And mark the outlet, and mark the relief and escape.

And as to you Corpse I think you are good manure, but that does
    not offend me,
I smell the white roses sweet-scented and growing,
I reach to the leafy lips, I reach to the polish'd breasts of melons.

And as to you Life I reckon you are the leavings of many deaths,
(No doubt I have died myself ten thousand times before.)

Earth, My Likeness

from I Sing the Body Electric

This is the female form,

A divine nimbus exhales from it from head to foot,

It attracts with fierce undeniable attraction,

I am drawn by its breath as if I were no more than a helpless vapor, all falls
   aside but myself and it,

Books, art, religion, time, the visible and solid earth, and what was expected
   of heaven or fear'd of hell, are now consumed,

Mad filaments, ungovernable shoots play out of it, the response likewise
   ungovernable,

Hair, bosom, hips, bend of legs, negligent falling hands all diffused,
   mine too diffused,

Ebb stung by the flow and flow stung by the ebb, love-flesh swelling and
   deliciously aching,

Limitless limpid jets of love hot and enormous, quivering jelly of love,
   white-blow and delirious juice,

Bridegroom night of love working surely and softly into the prostrate dawn,

Undulating into the willing and yielding day,

Lost in the cleave of the clasping and sweet-flesh'd day.

from I Sing the Body Electric

O my body! I dare not desert the likes of you in other men and
    women, nor the likes of the parts of you,
I believe the likes of you are to stand or fall with the likes of the soul,
    (and that they are the soul,)
I believe the likes of you are to stand or fall with my poems, and that
    they are my poems,
Man's, woman's, child's, youth's, wife's, husband's, mother's, father's,
    young man's, young woman's poems,
Head, neck, hair, ears, drop and tympan of the ears,
Eyes, eye-fringes, iris of the eye, eyebrows, and the waking or sleeping
    of the lids,
Mouth, tongue, lips, teeth, roof of mouth, jaws, and the jaw-hinges,
Nose, nostrils of the nose, and the partition,
Cheeks, temples, forehead, chin, throat, back of the neck, neck-slue,
Strong shoulders, manly beard, scapula, hind-shoulders, and the
    ample side-round of the chest,
Upper-arm, armpit, elbow-socket, lower-arm, arm-sinews, arm-bones,
Wrist and wrist-joints, hand, palm, knuckles, thumb, forefinger,
    finger-joints, finger-nails,
Broad breast-front, curling hair of the breast, breast-bone, breast-side,
Ribs, belly, backbone, joints of the backbone,
Hips, hip-sockets, hip-strength, inward and outward round, man-balls,
    man-root,
Strong set of thighs, well carrying the trunk above,
Leg-fibres, knee, knee-pan, upper-leg, under-leg,

Ankles, instep, foot-ball, toes, toe-joints, the heel;
All attitudes, all the shapeliness, all the belongings of my or your
    body or of any one's body, male or female,
The lung-sponges, the stomach-sac, the bowels sweet and clean,
The brain in its folds inside the skull-frame,
Sympathies, heart-valves, palate-valves, sexuality, maternity,
Womanhood, and all that is a woman, and the man that comes
    from woman,
The womb, the teats, nipples, breast-milk, tears, laughter, weeping,
    love-looks, love-perturbations and risings,
The voice, articulation, language, whispering, shouting aloud,
Food, drink, pulse, digestion, sweat, sleep, walking, swimming,
Poise on the hips, leaping, reclining, embracing, arm-curving
    and tightening,
The continual changes of the flex of the mouth, and around the eyes,
The skin, the sunburnt shade, freckles, hair,
The curious sympathy one feels when feeling with the hand the
    naked meat of the body,
The circling rivers the breath, and breathing it in and out,
The beauty of the waist, and thence of the hips, and thence
    downward toward the knees,
The thin red jellies within you or within me, the bones
    and the marrow in the bones,
The exquisite realization of health;
O I say these are not the parts and poems of the body only,
    but of the soul,
O I say now these are the soul!

Miracles

🍃 *from* Song of Myself

Do you guess I have some intricate purpose?
Well I have, for the Fourth-month showers have, and the mica
    on the side of a rock has.

Do you take it I would astonish?
Does the daylight astonish? does the early redstart twittering
    through the woods?
Do I astonish more than they?

This hour I tell things in confidence,
I might not tell everybody, but I will tell you.

NATURAL PERSONS

Give Me the Splendid Silent Sun

I

Give me the splendid silent sun with all his beams full-dazzling,
Give me juicy autumnal fruit ripe and red from the orchard,
Give me a field where the unmow'd grass grows,
Give me an arbor, give me the trellis'd grape,
Give me fresh corn and wheat, give me serene-moving animals teaching content,
Give me nights perfectly quiet as on high plateaus west of the Mississippi,
    and I looking up at the stars,
Give me odorous at sunrise the garden of beautiful flowers where I can walk
    undisturb'd,
Give me for marriage a sweet-breath'd woman of whom I should never tire,
Give me a perfect child, give me away aside from the noise of the world a rural
    domestic life,
Give me to warble spontaneous songs recluse by myself, for my own ears only,
Give me solitude, give me Nature, give me again O Nature your primal sanities!

These demanding to have them, (tired with ceaseless excitement, and rack'd
    by the war-strife,)
These to procure incessantly asking, rising in cries from my heart,
While yet incessantly asking still I adhere to my city,
Day upon day and year upon year O city, walking your streets,
Where you hold me enchain'd a certain time refusing to give me up,
Yet giving to make me glutted, enrich'd of soul, you give me forever faces;
(O I see what I sought to escape, confronting, reversing my cries,
I see my own soul trampling down what it ask'd for.)

2

Keep your splendid silent sun,

Keep your woods O Nature, and the quiet places by the woods,

Keep your fields of clover and timothy, and your corn-fields and orchards,

Keep the blossoming buckwheat fields where the Ninth-month bees hum,

Give me faces and streets—give me these phantoms incessant and endless along the trottoirs!

Give me interminable eyes—give me women—give me comrades and lovers by the thousand!

Let me see new ones every day—let me hold new ones by the hand every day!

Give me such shows—give me the streets of Manhattan!

Give me Broadway, with the soldiers marching—give me the sound of the trumpets and drums!

(The soldiers in companies or regiments—some starting away, flush'd and reckless,

Some, their time up, returning with thinn'd ranks, young, yet very old, worn, marching, noticing nothing;)

Give me the shores and wharves heavy-fringed with black ships!

O such for me! O an intense life, full to repletion and varied!

The life of the theatre, bar-room, huge hotel, for me!

The saloon of the steamer! the crowded excursion for me! the torchlight procession!

The dense brigade bound for the war, with high piled military wagons following;

People, endless, streaming, with strong voices, passions, pageants,

Manhattan streets with their powerful throbs, with beating drums as now,

The endless and noisy chorus, the rustle and clank of muskets, (even the sight of the wounded,)

Manhattan crowds, with their turbulent musical chorus!

Manhattan faces and eyes forever for me.

Earth, My Likeness

from A Song of Joys

O to have been brought up on bays, lagoons, creeks, or along the coast,

To continue and be employ'd there all my life,

The briny and damp smell, the shore, the salt weeds exposed at low water,

The work of fishermen, the work of the eel-fisher and clam-fisher;

I come with my clam-rake and spade, I come with my eel-spear,

Is the tide out? I join the group of clam-diggers on the flats,

I laugh and work with them, I joke at my work like a mettlesome young man;

In winter I take my eel-basket and eel-spear and travel out on foot on the
    ice—I have a small axe to cut holes in the ice,

Behold me well-clothed going gayly or returning in the afternoon, my brood
    of tough boys accompanying me,

My brood of grown and part-grown boys,
    who love to be with no one else so well as
    they love to be with me,

By day to work with me, and by night to
    sleep with me.

from Our Old Feuillage

The camp of Georgia wagoners just after dark, the supper-fires and the
    cooking and eating by whites and negroes,
Thirty or forty great wagons, the mules, cattle, horses, feeding from troughs,
The shadows, gleams, up under the leaves of the old sycamore-trees, the
    flames with the black smoke from the pitch-pine curling and rising...

from Song of Myself

The boatmen and clam-diggers arose early and stopt for me,
I tuck'd my trowser-ends in my boots and went and had a good time;
You should have been with us that day round the chowder-kettle.

from Song of Myself

The negro holds firmly the reins of his four horses, the block swags
    underneath on its tied-over chain,
The negro that drives the long dray of the stone-yard, steady and tall
    he stands pois'd on one leg on the string-piece,
His blue shirt exposes his ample neck and breast and loosens over
    his hip-band,
His glance is calm and commanding, he tosses the slouch of his hat
    away from his forehead,
The sun falls on his crispy hair and mustache, falls on the black of
    his polish'd and perfect limbs.

Earth, My Likeness

from The Sleepers

Now what my mother told me one day as we sat at dinner together,
Of when she was a nearly grown girl living with her parents
    on the old homestead.

A red squaw came one breakfast-time to the old homestead,
On her back she carried a bundle of rushes for rush-bottoming chairs,
Her hair, straight, shiny, coarse, black, profuse, half-envelop'd her face,
Her step was free and elastic, and her voice sounded exquisitely
    as she spoke.

My mother look'd in delight and amazement at the stranger,
She look'd at the freshness of her tall-borne face and full and pliant limbs,
The more she look'd upon her she loved her,
Never before had she seen such wonderful beauty and purity,
She made her sit on a bench by the jamb of the fireplace, she cook'd food
    for her,
She had no work to give her, but she gave her remembrance and fondness.

The red squaw staid all the forenoon, and toward the middle of the
    afternoon she went away,
O my mother was loth to have her go away,
All the week she thought of her, she watch'd for her many a month,
She remember'd her many a winter and many a summer,
But the red squaw never came nor was heard of there again.

Abraham Lincoln

August 12th.—I see the President almost every day, as I happen to live where he passes to or from his lodgings out of town. He never sleeps at the White House during the hot season, but has quarters at a healthy location some three miles north of the city, the Soldiers' home, a United States military establishment. I saw him this morning about 8 1/2 coming in to business, riding on Vermont avenue, near L street. He always has a company of twenty-five or thirty cavalry, with sabres drawn and held upright over their shoulders. They say this guard was against his personal wish, but he let his counselors have their way. The party makes no great show in uniform or horses. Mr. Lincoln on the saddle generally rides a good-sized, easy-going gray horse, is dress'd in plain black, somewhat rusty and dusty, wears a black stiff hat, and looks about as ordinary in attire, &c., as the commonest man.... I see very plainly Abraham Lincoln's dark brown face, with deep-cut lines, the eyes, always to me with a deep latent sadness in the expression. We have got so that we exchange bows, and very cordial ones.... Earlier in the summer I occasionally saw the President and his wife, toward the latter part of the afternoon, out in a barouche, on a pleasure ride through the city. Mrs. Lincoln was dress'd in complete black, with a long crape veil. The equipage is of the plainest kind, only two horses, and they nothing extra. They pass'd me once very close, and I saw the President in the face fully, as they were moving slowly, and his look, though abstracted, happen'd to be directed steadily in my eye. He bow'd and smiled, but far beneath his smile I noticed well the expression I have alluded to. None of the artists or pictures has caught the deep, though subtle and indirect expression of this man's face. There is something else there. One of the great portrait painters of two or three centuries ago is needed.

A Specimen Tramp Family

June 22.—This afternoon we went out (J. B., Al. and I) on quite a drive around the country. The scenery, the perpetual stone fences, (some venerable old fellows, dark-spotted with lichens)—the many fine locust-trees—the runs of brawling water, often over descents of rock—these, and lots else. It is lucky the roads are first-rate here, (as they are,) for it is up or down hill everywhere, and sometimes steep enough. B. has a tip-top horse, strong, young, and both gentle and fast. There is a great deal of waste land and hills on the river edge of Ulster county, with a wonderful luxuriance of wild flowers and bushes—and it seems to me I never saw more vitality of trees—eloquent hemlocks, plenty of locusts and fine maples, and the balm of Gilead, giving out aroma. In the fields and along the road-sides unusual crops of the tall-stemm'd wild daisy, white as milk and yellow as gold.

We pass'd quite a number of tramps, singly or in couples—one squad, a family in a rickety one-horse wagon, with some baskets evidently their work and trade—the man seated on a low board, in front, driving—the gauntish woman by his side, with a baby well bundled in her arms, its little red feet and lower legs sticking out right towards us as we pass'd—and in the wagon behind, we saw two (or three) crouching little children. It was a queer, taking, rather sad picture. If I had been alone and on foot, I should have stopp'd and held confab. But on our return nearly two hours afterward, we found them a ways further along the same road, in a lonesome open spot, haul'd aside, unhitch'd, and evidently going to camp for the night. The freed horse was not far off, quietly cropping the grass. The man was busy at the wagon, the boy had gather'd some dry wood, and was making a fire—and as we went a little further we met the woman afoot. I could not see her face, in its great sun-bonnet, but somehow her figure and gait told misery, terror, destitution. She had the rag-bundled, half-starv'd infant still in her arms, and in her hands held two or three baskets, which she had evidently taken to the next house for sale. A little barefoot five-year old girl-child, with fine eyes, trotted behind her, clutching her gown. We stopp'd, asking about the baskets, which we bought. As we paid the money, she kept her face hidden in the recesses of her bonnet. Then as we started, and stopp'd again, Al., (whose sympathies were evidently arous'd,) went back to the camping group to get another basket. He caught a look of her face, and talk'd with her a little. Eyes, voice and manner were those of a corpse, animated by electricity. She was quite young—the man she was traveling with, middle-aged. Poor woman—what story was it, out of her fortunes, to account for that inexpressibly scared way, those glassy eyes, and that hollow voice?

Earth, My Likeness

Meeting a Hermit

I found in one of my rambles up the hills a real hermit, living in a lonesome spot, hard to get at, rocky, the view fine, with a little patch of land two rods square. A man of youngish middle age, city born and raised, had been to school, had travel'd in Europe and California. I first met him once or twice on the road, and pass'd the time of day, with some small talk; then, the third time, he ask'd me to go along a bit and rest in his hut (an almost unprecedented compliment, as I heard from others afterwards.) He was of Quaker stock, I think; talk'd with ease and moderate freedom, but did not unbosom his life, or story, or tragedy, or whatever it was.

The Runner

On a flat road runs the well-train'd runner,
He is lean and sinewy with muscular legs,
He is thinly clothed, he leans forward as he runs,
With lightly closed fists and arms partially rais'd.

Beautiful Women

Women sit or move to and fro, some old, some young,
The young are beautiful—but the old are more beautiful than the young.

from I Sing the Body Electric

I knew a man, a common farmer, the father of five sons,
And in them the fathers of sons, and in them the fathers of sons.

This man was of wonderful vigor, calmness, beauty of person,
The shape of his head, the pale yellow and white of his hair and beard, the
    immeasurable meaning of his black eyes, the richness and breadth of his
    manners,
These I used to go and visit him to see, he was wise also,
He was six feet tall, he was over eighty years old, his sons were massive,
    clean, bearded, tan-faced, handsome,
They and his daughters loved him, all who saw him loved him,
They did not love him by allowance, they loved him with personal love,
He drank water only, the blood show'd like scarlet through the clear-brown
    skin of his face,
He was a frequent gunner and fisher, he sail'd his boat himself, he had a fine
    one presented him by a ship-joiner, he had fowling pieces presented to
    him by men that loved him,
When he went with his five sons and many grand-sons to hunt or fish, you
    would pick him out as the most beautiful and vigorous of the gang,
You would wish long and long to be with him, you would wish to sit by him
    in the boat that you might touch each other.

Hot Weather, New York

Aug. 10.—As I haltingly ramble an hour or two this forenoon by the more secluded parts of the shore, or sit under an old cedar half way up the hill, the city near in view, many young parties gather to bathe or swim, squads of boys, generally twos or threes, some larger ones, along the sand-bottom, or off an old pier close by. A peculiar and pretty carnival—at its height a hundred lads or young men, very democratic, but all decent behaving. The laughter, voices, calls, responses—the springing and diving of the bathers from the great string-piece of the decay'd pier, where climb or stand long ranks of them, naked, rose-color'd, with movements, postures ahead of any sculpture. To all this, the sun, so bright, the dark-green shadow of the hills the other side, the amber-rolling waves, changing as the tide comes in to a transparent tea-color—the frequent splash of the playful boys, sousing—the glittering drops sparkling, and the good western breeze blowing.

Natural Persons

from Song of Myself

Twenty-eight young men bathe by the shore,
Twenty-eight young men and all so friendly;
Twenty-eight years of womanly life and all so lonesome.

She owns the fine house by the rise of the bank,
She hides handsome and richly drest aft the blinds of the window.

Which of the young men does she like the best?
Ah the homeliest of them is beautiful to her.

Where are you off to, lady? for I see you,
You splash in the water there, yet stay stock still in your room.

Dancing and laughing along the beach came the twenty-ninth bather,
The rest did not see her, but she saw them and loved them.

The beards of the young men glisten'd with wet, it ran from their long hair,
Little streams pass'd all over their bodies.

An unseen hand also pass'd over their bodies,
It descended tremblingly from their temples and ribs.

The young men float on their backs, their white bellies bulge to the sun,
    they do not ask who seizes fast to them,
They do not know who puffs and declines with pendant and bending arch,
They do not think whom they souse with spray.

from A Song for Occupations

When the psalm sings instead of the singer,
When the script preaches instead of the preacher,
When the pulpit descends and goes instead of the carver
    that carved the supporting desk,
When I can touch the body of books by night or by day,
    and when they touch my body back again,
When a university course convinces like a slumbering
    woman and child convince,
When the minted gold in the vault smiles like the night-
    watchman's daughter,
When warrantee deeds loafe in chairs opposite and are
    my friendly companions,
I intend to reach them my hand, and make as much of
    them as I do of men and women like you.

THE SEA

Out of the Cradle Endlessly Rocking

Out of the cradle endlessly rocking,
Out of the mocking-bird's throat, the musical shuttle,
Out of the Ninth-month midnight,
Over the sterile sands and the fields beyond, where the child leaving
    his bed wander'd alone, bareheaded, barefoot,
Down from the shower'd halo,
Up from the mystic play of shadows twining and twisting as if they
    were alive,
Out from the patches of briers and blackberries,
From the memories of the bird that chanted to me,
From your memories sad brother, from the fitful risings and fallings I heard,
From under that yellow half-moon late-risen and swollen as if with tears,
From those beginning notes of yearning and love there in the mist,
From the thousand responses of my heart never to cease,
From the myriad thence-arous'd words,
From the word stronger and more delicious than any,
From such as now they start the scene revisiting,
As a flock, twittering, rising, or overhead passing,
Borne hither, ere all eludes me, hurriedly,
A man, yet by these tears a little boy again,
Throwing myself on the sand, confronting the waves,
I, chanter of pains and joys, uniter of here and hereafter,
Taking all hints to use them, but swiftly leaping beyond them,
A reminiscence sing.

Once Paumanok,

When the lilac-scent was in the air and Fifth-month grass was growing,

Up this seashore in some briers,

Two feather'd guests from Alabama, two together,

And their nest, and four light-green eggs spotted with brown,

And every day the he-bird to and fro near at hand,

And every day the she-bird crouch'd on her nest, silent, with bright eyes,

And every day I, a curious boy, never too close, never disturbing them,

Cautiously peering, absorbing, translating.

Shine! shine! shine!
Pour down your warmth, great sun!
While we bask, we two together.

Two together!
Winds blow south, or winds blow north,
Day come white, or night come black,
Home, or rivers and mountains from home,
Singing all time, minding no time,
While we two keep together.

Till of a sudden,

May-be kill'd, unknown to her mate,

One forenoon the she-bird crouch'd not on the nest,

Nor return'd that afternoon, nor the next,

Nor ever appear'd again.

And thenceforward all summer in the sound of the sea,

And at night under the full moon in calmer weather,

Over the hoarse surging of the sea,

Or flitting from brier to brier by day,
I saw, I heard at intervals the remaining one, the he-bird,
The solitary guest from Alabama.

Blow! blow! blow!
Blow up sea-winds along Paumanok's shore;
I wait and I wait till you blow my mate to me.

Yes, when the stars glisten'd,
All night long on the prong of a moss-scallop'd stake,
Down almost amid the slapping waves,
Sat the lone singer wonderful causing tears.

He call'd on his mate,
He pour'd forth the meanings which I of all men know.

Yes my brother I know,
The rest might not, but I have treasur'd every note,
For more than once dimly down to the beach gliding,
Silent, avoiding the moonbeams, blending myself with the shadows,
Recalling now the obscure shapes, the echoes, the sounds and sights
    after their sorts,
The white arms out in the breakers tirelessly tossing,
I, with bare feet, a child, the wind wafting my hair,
Listen'd long and long.

Listen'd to keep, to sing, now translating the notes,
Following you my brother.

Soothe! soothe! soothe!
Close on its waves soothes the wave behind,
And again another behind embracing and lapping, every one close,
But my love soothes not me, not me.

Low hangs the moon, it rose late,
It is lagging—O I think it is heavy with love, with love.

O madly the sea pushes upon the land,
With love, with love.

O night! do I not see my love fluttering out among the breakers?
What is that little black thing I see there in the white?

Loud! loud! loud!
Loud I call to you, my love!

High and clear I shoot my voice over the waves,
Surely you must know who is here, is here,
You must know who I am, my love.

Low-hanging moon!
What is that dusky spot in your brown yellow?
O it is the shape, the shape of my mate!
O moon do not keep her from me any longer.

Land! land! O land!
Whichever way I turn, O I think you could give me my mate back again
    if you only would,
For I am almost sure I see her dimly whichever way I look.

Earth, My Likeness

O rising stars!
Perhaps the one I want so much will rise, will rise with some of you.

O throat! O trembling throat!
Sound clearer through the atmosphere!
Pierce the woods, the earth,
Somewhere listening to catch you must be the one I want.

Shake out carols!
Solitary here, the night's carols!
Carols under the lagging, yellow, waning moon!
O under the moon where she droops almost down into the sea!
O reckless despairing carols.

But soft! sink low!
Soft! let me just murmur,
And do you wait a moment you husky-nois'd sea,
For somewhere I believe I heard my mate responding to me,
So faint, I must be still, be still to listen,
But not altogether still, for then she might not come immediately to me.

Hither my love!
Here I am! here!
With this just-sustain'd note I announce myself to you,
This gentle call is for you my love, for you.

Do not be decoy'd elsewhere,
That is the whistle of the wind, it is not my voice,
That is the fluttering, the fluttering of the spray,
Those are the shadows of leaves.

The Sea

O darkness! O in vain!
O I am very sick and sorrowful.

O brown halo in the sky near the moon, drooping upon the sea!
O troubled reflection in the sea!
O throat! O throbbing heart!
And I singing uselessly, uselessly all the night.

O past! O happy life! O songs of joy!
In the air, in the woods, over fields,
Loved! loved! loved! loved! loved!
But my mate no more, no more with me!
We two together no more.

The aria sinking,
All else continuing, the stars shining,
The winds blowing, the notes of the bird continuous echoing,
With angry moans the fierce old mother incessantly moaning,
On the sands of Paumanok's shore gray and rustling,
The yellow half-moon enlarged, sagging down, drooping, the face of the sea
    almost touching,
The boy ecstatic, with his bare feet the waves, with his hair the atmosphere
    dallying,
The love in the heart long pent, now loose, now at last tumultuously bursting,
The aria's meaning, the ears, the soul, swiftly depositing,
The strange tears down the cheeks coursing,
The colloquy there, the trio, each uttering,
The undertone, the savage old mother incessantly crying,
To the boy's soul's questions sullenly timing, some drown'd secret hissing,
To the outsetting bard.

Demon or bird! (said the boy's soul,)

Is it indeed toward your mate you sing? or is it really to me?

For I, that was a child, my tongue's use sleeping, now I have heard you,

Now in a moment I know what I am for, I awake,

And already a thousand singers, a thousand songs, clearer, louder and
    more sorrowful than yours,

A thousand warbling echoes have started to life within me, never to die.

O you singer solitary, singing by yourself, projecting me,

O solitary me listening, never more shall I cease perpetuating you,

Never more shall I escape, never more the reverberations,

Never more the cries of unsatisfied love be absent from me,

Never again leave me to be the peaceful child I was before what there
    in the night,

By the sea under the yellow and sagging moon,

The messenger there arous'd, the fire, the sweet hell within,

The unknown want, the destiny of me.

O give me the clew! (it lurks in the night here somewhere,)

O if I am to have so much, let me have more!

A word then, (for I will conquer it,)

The word final, superior to all,

Subtle, sent up—what is it?—I listen;

Are you whispering it, and have been all the time, you sea-waves?

Is that it from your liquid rims and wet sands?

Whereto answering, the sea,

Delaying not, hurrying not,

Whisper'd me through the night, and very plainly before day-break,

Lisp'd to me the low and delicious word death,

And again death, death, death, death,

Hissing melodious, neither like the bird nor like my arous'd child's heart,

But edging near as privately for me rustling at my feet,

Creeping thence steadily up to my ears and laving me softly all over,

Death, death, death, death, death.

Which I do not forget,

But fuse the song of my dusky demon and brother,

That he sang to me in the moonlight on Paumanok's gray beach,

With the thousand responsive songs at random,

My own songs awaked from that hour,

And with them the key, the word up from the waves,

The word of the sweetest song and all songs,

That strong and delicious word which, creeping to my feet,

(Or like some old crone rocking the cradle, swathed in sweet garments,
    bending aside,)

The sea whisper'd me.

from Song of Myself

You sea! I resign myself to you also—I guess what you mean,
I behold from the beach your crooked inviting fingers,
I believe you refuse to go back without feeling of me,
We must have a turn together, I undress, hurry me out of sight of the land,
Cushion me soft, rock me in billowy drowse,
Dash me with amorous wet, I can repay you.

from The Sleepers

The beach is cut by the razory ice-wind, the wreck-
    guns sound,
The tempest lulls, the moon comes floundering
    through the drifts.

I look where the ship helplessly heads end on, I hear
    the burst as she strikes, I hear the howls of dismay,
    they grow fainter and fainter.

I cannot aid with my wringing fingers,
I can but rush to the surf and let it drench me and
    freeze upon me.

I search with the crowd, not one of the company is
    wash'd to us alive,
In the morning I help pick up the dead and lay them
    in rows in a barn.

from As I Ebb'd with the Ocean of Life

As I wend to the shores I know not,
As I list to the dirge, the voices of men and women wreck'd,
As I inhale the impalpable breezes that set in upon me,
As the ocean so mysterious rolls toward me closer and closer,
I too but signify at the utmost a little wash'd up drift,
A few sands and dead leaves to gather,
Gather, and merge myself as part of the sands and drift.

O baffled, balk'd to the very earth,
Oppress'd with myself that I have dared to open my mouth,
Aware now that amid all that blab whose echoes recoil upon me I have not
    once had the least idea who or what I am,
But that before all my arrogant poems the real Me stands yet untouch'd,
    untold, altogether unreach'd,
Withdrawn far, mocking me with mock-congratulatory signs and bows,
With peals of distant ironical laughter at every word I have written,
Pointing in silence to these songs, and then to the sand beneath.

I perceive I have not really understood any thing, not a single object,
    and that no man ever can,
Nature here in sight of the sea taking advantage of me to dart upon me
    and sting me,
Because I have dared to open my mouth to sing at all.

The Sea

The World Below the Brine

The world below the brine,
Forests at the bottom of the sea, the branches and leaves,
Sea-lettuce, vast lichens, strange flowers and seeds, the thick tangle,
    openings, and pink turf,
Different colors, pale gray and green, purple, white, and gold, the play
    of light through the water,
Dumb swimmers there among the rocks, coral, gluten, grass, rushes,
    and the aliment of the swimmers,
Sluggish existences grazing there suspended, or slowly crawling close
    to the bottom,
The sperm-whale at the surface blowing air and spray, or disporting
    with his flukes,
The leaden-eyed shark, the walrus, the turtle, the hairy sea-leopard,
    and the sting-ray,
Passions there, wars, pursuits, tribes, sight in those ocean-depths,
    breathing that thick-breathing air, as so many do,
The change thence to the sight here, and to the subtle air breathed by
    beings like us who walk this sphere,
The change onward from ours to that of beings who walk other spheres.

A Paumanok Picture

Two boats with nets lying off the sea-beach, quite still,
Ten fishermen waiting—they discover a thick school of mossbonkers—
   they drop the join'd seine-ends in the water,
The boats separate and row off, each on its rounding course to the beach,
   enclosing the mossbonkers,
The net is drawn in by a windlass by those who stop ashore,
Some of the fishermen lounge in their boats, others stand ankle-deep
   in the water, pois'd on strong legs,
The boats partly drawn up, the water slapping against them,
Strew'd on the sand in heaps and windrows, well out from the water,
   the green-back'd spotted mossbunkers.

Sea-Shore Fancies

Even as a boy, I had the fancy, the wish, to write a piece, perhaps a poem, about the sea-shore—that suggesting, dividing line, contact, junction, the solid marrying the liquid—that curious, lurking something, (as doubtless every objective form finally becomes to the subjective spirit,) which means far more than its mere first sight, grand as that is—blending the real and ideal, and each made portion of the other. Hours, days, in my Long Island youth and early manhood, I haunted the shores of Rockaway or Coney island, or away east to the Hamptons or Montauk. Once, at the latter place, (by the old lighthouse, nothing but sea-tossings in sight in every direction as far as the eye could reach,) I remember well, I felt that I must one day write a book expressing this liquid, mystic theme. Afterward, I recollect, how it came to me that instead of any special lyrical or epical or literary attempt, the sea-shore should be an invisible *influence*, a pervading gauge and tally for me, in my composition. (Let me give a hint here to young writers. I am not sure but I have unwittingly follow'd out the same rule with other powers besides sea and shores—avoiding them, in the way of any dead set at poetizing them, as too big for formal handling—quite satisfied if I could indirectly show that we have met and fused, even if only once, but enough—that we have really absorb'd each other and understand each other.)

There is a dream, a picture, that for years at intervals, (sometimes quite long ones, but surely again, in time,) has come noiselessly up before me, and I really believe, fiction as it is, has enter'd largely into my practical life—certainly into my writings, and shaped and color'd them. It is nothing more or less than a stretch of interminable white-brown sand, hard and smooth and broad, with the ocean perpetually, grandly, rolling in upon it, with slow-measured sweep, with rustle and hiss and foam, and many a thump as of low bass drums. This scene, this picture, I say, has risen before me at times for years. Sometimes I wake at night and can hear and see it plainly.

🪶 A Winter Day on the Sea-Beach

One bright December mid-day lately I spent down on the New Jersey sea-shore, reaching it by a little more than an hour's railroad trip over the old Camden and Atlantic. I had started betimes, fortified by nice strong coffee and a good breakfast (cook'd by the hands I love, my dear sister Lou's—how much better it makes the victuals taste, and then assimilate, strengthen you, perhaps make the whole day comfortable afterwards.) Five or six miles at the last, our track enter'd a broad region of salt grass meadows, intersected by lagoons, and cut up everywhere by watery runs. The sedgy perfume, delightful to my nostrils, reminded me of "the mash" and south bay of my native island. I could have journey'd contentedly till night through these flat and odorous sea-prairies. From half past 11 till 2 I was nearly all the time along the beach, or in sight of the ocean, listening to its hoarse murmur, and inhaling the bracing and welcome breezes. First, a rapid five-mile drive over the hard sand—our carriage wheels hardly made dents in it. Then after dinner (as there were nearly two hours to spare) I walk'd off in another direction, (hardly met or saw a person,) and taking possession of what appear'd to have been the reception-room of an old bath-house range, had a broad expanse of view all to myself—quaint, refreshing, unimpeded—a dry area of sedge and Indian grass immediately before and around me—space, simple, unornamented space. Distant vessels, and the far-off, just visible trailing smoke of an inward bound steamer; more plainly, ships, brigs, schooners, in sight, most of them with every sail set to the firm and steady wind.

The attractions, fascinations there are in sea and shore! How one dwells on their simplicity, even vacuity! What is it in us, arous'd by those indirections and directions? That spread of waves and gray-white beach, salt, monotonous, senseless—such an entire absence of art, books, talk, elegance—so indescribably comforting, even this winter day—grim, yet so delicate-looking, so spiritual—

striking emotional, impalpable depths, subtler than all the poems, paintings, music, I have ever read, seen, heard. (Yet let me be fair, perhaps it is because I have read those poems and heard that music.)

Had I the Choice

Had I the choice to tally greatest bards,
To limn their portraits, stately, beautiful, and
    emulate at will,
Homer with all his wars and warriors—Hector,
    Achilles, Ajax,
Or Shakspere's woe-entangled Hamlet, Lear,
    Othello—Tennyson's fair ladies,
Metre or wit the best, or choice conceit to wield
    in perfect rhyme, delight of singers;
These, these, O sea, all these I'd gladly barter,
Would you the undulation of one wave, its
    trick to me transfer,
Or breathe one breath of yours upon my verse,
And leave its odor there.

HERBAGE and COMRADES

These I Singing in Spring

These I singing in spring collect for lovers,

(For who but I should understand lovers and all their sorrow and joy?

And who but I should be the poet of comrades?)

Collecting I traverse the garden of the world, but soon I pass the gates,

Now along the pond-side, now wading in a little, fearing not the wet,

Now by the post-and-rail fences where the old stones thrown there, pick'd
   from the fields, have accumulated,

(Wild-flowers and vines and weeds come up through the stones and partly
   cover them, beyond these I pass,)

Far, far in the forest, or sauntering later in the summer, before I think where
   I go,

Solitary, smelling the earthy smell, stopping now and then in the silence,

Alone I had thought, yet soon a troop gathers around me,

Some walk by my side and some behind, and some embrace my arms or neck,

They the spirits of dear friends dead or alive, thicker they come, a great
   crowd, and I in the middle,

Collecting, dispensing, singing, there I wander with them,

Plucking something for tokens, tossing toward whoever is near me,

Here, lilac, with a branch of pine,

Here, out of my pocket, some moss which I pull'd off a live-oak in Florida
   as it hung trailing down,

Here, some pinks and laurel leaves, and a handful of sage,

And here what I now draw from the water, wading in the pond-side,

(O here I last saw him that tenderly loves me, and returns again never to
   separate from me,

And this, O this shall henceforth be the token of comrades, this calamus-
   root shall,

Interchange it youths with each other! let none render it back!)
And twigs of maple and a bunch of wild orange and chestnut,
And stems of currants and plum-blows, and the aromatic cedar,
These I compass'd around by a thick cloud of spirits,
Wandering, point to or touch as I pass, or throw them loosely from me,
Indicating to each one what he shall have, giving something to each;
But what I drew from the water by the pond-side, that I reserve,
I will give of it, but only to them that love as I myself am capable of loving.

I Saw in Louisiana a Live-Oak Growing

I saw in Louisiana a live-oak growing,
All alone stood it and the moss hung down from the branches,
Without any companion it grew there uttering joyous leaves of dark green,
And its look, rude, unbending, lusty, made me think of myself,
But I wonder'd how it could utter joyous leaves standing alone there
    without its friend near, for I knew I could not,
And I broke off a twig with a certain number of leaves upon it, and twined
    around it a little moss,
And brought it away, and I have placed it in sight in my room,
It is not needed to remind me as of my own dear friends,
(For I believe lately I think of little else than of them,)
Yet it remains to me a curious token, it makes me think of manly love;
For all that, and though the live-oak glistens there in Louisiana solitary
    in a wide flat space,
Uttering joyous leaves all its life without a friend a lover near,
I know very well I could not.

We Two Boys Together Clinging

We two boys together clinging,
One the other never leaving,
Up and down the roads going, North and South excursions making,
Power enjoying, elbows stretching, fingers clutching,
Arm'd and fearless, eating, drinking, sleeping, loving,
No law less than ourselves owning, sailing, soldiering, thieving, threatening,
Misers, menials, priests alarming, air breathing, water drinking, on the turf
   or the sea-beach dancing,
Cities wrenching, ease scorning, statutes mocking, feebleness chasing,
Fulfilling our foray.

from Song of Myself

Loafe with me on the grass, loose the stop from your throat,
Not words, not music or rhyme I want, nor custom or lecture, not
    even the best,
Only the lull I like, the hum of your valved voice.

I mind how once we lay such a transparent summer morning,
How you settled your head athwart my hips and gently turn'd over
    upon me,
And parted the shirt from my bosom-bone, and plunged your tongue
    to my bare-stript heart,
And reach'd till you felt my beard, and reach'd till you held my feet.

Swiftly arose and spread around me the peace and knowledge that
    pass all the argument of the earth,
And I know that the hand of God is the promise of my own,
And I know that the spirit of God is the brother of my own,
And that all the men ever born are also my brothers, and the women
    my sisters and lovers,
And that a kelson of the creation is love,
And limitless are leaves stiff or drooping in the fields,
And brown ants in the little wells beneath them,
And mossy scabs of the worm fence, heap'd stones, elder, mullein,
    and poke-weed.

Mulleins and Mulleins

Large, placid mulleins, as summer advances, velvety in texture, of a light greenish-drab color, growing everywhere in the fields—at first earth's big rosettes in their broad-leav'd low cluster-plants, eight, ten, twenty leaves to a plant—plentiful on the fallow twenty-acre lot, at the end of the lane, and especially by the ridge-sides of the fences—then close to the ground, but soon springing up—leaves as broad as my hand, and the lower ones twice as long—so fresh and dewy in the morning—stalks now four or five, even seven or eight feet high. The farmers, I find, think the mullein a mean unworthy weed, but I have grown to a fondness for it. Every object has its lesson, enclosing the suggestion of everything else—and lately I sometimes think all is concentrated for me in these hardy, yellow-flower'd weeds. As I come down the lane early in the morning, I pause before their soft wool-like fleece and stem and broad leaves, glittering with countless diamonds. Annually for three summers now, they and I have silently return'd together; at such long intervals I stand or sit among them, musing—and woven with the rest, of so many hours and moods of partial rehabilitation—of my sane or sick spirit, here as near at peace as it can be.

The Oaks and I

Sept. 5, '77.—I write this, 11 A.M., shelter'd under a dense oak by the bank, where I have taken refuge from a sudden rain. I came down here, (we had sulky drizzles all the morning, but an hour ago a lull,) for the before-mention'd daily and simple exercise I am fond of—to pull on that young hickory sapling out there—to sway and yield to its tough-limber upright stem—haply to get into my old sinews some of its elastic fibre and clear sap. I stand on the turf and take these health-pulls moderately and at intervals for nearly an hour, inhaling great draughts of fresh air. Wandering by the creek, I have three or four naturally favorable spots where I rest—besides a chair I lug with me and use for more deliberate occasions. At other spots convenient I have selected, besides the hickory just named, strong and limber boughs of beech or holly, in easy-reaching distance, for my natural gymnasia, for arms, chest, trunk-muscles. I can soon feel the sap and sinew rising through me, like mercury to heat. I hold on boughs or slender trees caressingly there in the sun and shade, wrestle with their innocent stalwartness—and *know* the virtue thereof passes from them into me. (Or may-be we interchange—may-be the trees are more aware of it all than I ever thought.)

from The Lesson of a Tree

Aug. 4, 6 P.M.—Lights and shades and rare effects on tree-foliage and grass— transparent greens, grays, &c., all in sunset pomp and dazzle. The clear beams are now thrown in many new places, on the quilted, seam'd, bronze-drab, lower tree-trunks, shadow'd except at this hour—now flooding their young and columnar ruggedness with strong light, unfolding to my sense new amazing features of silent, shaggy charm, the solid bark, the expression of harmless impassiveness, with many a bulge and gnarl unreck'd before. In the revealings of such light, such exceptional hour, such mood, one does not wonder at the old story fables, (indeed, why fables?) of people falling into love-sickness with trees, seiz'd extatic with the mystic realism of the resistless silent strength in them—*strength,* which after all is perhaps the last, completest, highest beauty.

Roots and Leaves Themselves Alone

Roots and leaves themselves alone are these,
Scents brought to me and women from the wild woods and pond-side,
Breast-sorrel and pinks of love, fingers that wind around tighter than vines,
Gushes from the throats of birds hid in the foliage of trees as the sun is risen,
Breezes of land and love set from living shores to you on the living sea, to
    you O sailors!

Earth, My Likeness

Frost-mellow'd berries and Third-month twigs offer'd fresh to young persons
    wandering out in the fields when the winter breaks up,
Love-buds put before you and within you whoever you are,
Buds to be unfolded on the old terms,
If you bring the warmth of the sun to them they will open and bring form,
    color, perfume, to you,
If you become the aliment and the wet they will become flowers, fruits, tall
    branches and trees.

A Night Remembrance

Aug. 25, 9–10 A.M.—I sit by the edge of the pond, everything quiet, the broad polish'd surface spread before me—the blue of the heavens and the white clouds reflected from it—and flitting across, now and then, the reflection of some flying bird. Last night I was down here with a friend till after midnight; everything a miracle of splendor—the glory of the stars, and the completely rounded moon—the passing clouds, silver and luminous-tawny—now and then masses of vapory illuminated scud—and silently by my side my dear friend. The shades of the trees, and patches of moonlight on the grass—a softly blowing breeze, and just-palpable odor of the neighboring ripening corn—the indolent and spiritual night, inexpressibly rich, tender, suggestive—something altogether to filter through one's soul, and nourish and feed and soothe the memory long afterwards.

from When Lilacs Last in the Dooryard Bloom'd

Coffin that passes through lanes and streets,

Through day and night with the great cloud darkening the land,

With the pomp of the inloop'd flags with the cities draped in black,

With the show of the States themselves as of crape-veil'd women standing,

With processions long and winding and the flambeaus of the night,

With the countless torches lit, with the silent sea of faces and the unbared heads,

With the waiting depot, the arriving coffin, and the sombre faces,

With dirges through the night, with the thousand voices rising strong and solemn,

With all the mournful voices of the dirges pour'd around the coffin,

The dim-lit churches and the shuddering organs—where amid these you journey,

With the tolling tolling bells' perpetual clang,

Here, coffin that slowly passes,

I give you my sprig of lilac.

(Nor for you, for one alone,

Blossoms and branches green to coffins all I bring,

For fresh as the morning, thus would I chant a song for you O sane
    and sacred death.

All over bouquets of roses,

O death, I cover you over with roses and early lilies,

But mostly and now the lilac that blooms the first,

Copious I break, I break the sprigs from the bushes,

With loaded arms I come, pouring for you,

For you and the coffins all of you O death.)

Earth, My Likeness

Earth, my likeness,

Though you look so impassive, ample and spheric there,

I now suspect that is not all;

I now suspect there is something fierce in you eligible to burst forth,

For an athlete is enamor'd of me, and I of him,

But toward him there is something fierce and terrible in me eligible
   to burst forth,

I dare not tell it in words, not even in these songs.

Spontaneous Me

Spontaneous me, Nature,

The loving day, the mounting sun, the friend I am happy with,

The arm of my friend hanging idly over my shoulder,

The hillside whiten'd with blossoms of the mountain ash,

The same late in autumn, the hues of red, yellow, drab, purple, and light and
dark green,

The rich coverlet of the grass, animals and birds, the private untrimm'd bank,
the primitive apples, the pebble-stones,

Beautiful dripping fragments, the negligent list of one after another as I
happen to call them to me or think of them,

The real poems, (what we call poems being merely pictures,)

The poems of the privacy of the night, and of men like me,

This poem drooping shy and unseen that I always carry, and that all men carry,

(Know once for all, avow'd on purpose, wherever are men like me, are our
lusty lurking masculine poems,)

Love-thoughts, love-juice, love-odor, love-yielding, love-climbers, and the
climbing sap,

Arms and hands of love, lips of love, phallic thumb of love, breasts of love,
bellies press'd and glued together with love,

Earth of chaste love, the body of the woman I love, the body of the man,
the body of the earth,

Soft forenoon airs that blow from the south-west,

The hairy wild-bee that murmurs and hankers up and down, that gripes the
full-grown lady-flower, curves upon her with amorous firm legs, takes his
will of her, and holds himself tremulous and tight till he is satisfied;

The wet of woods through the early hours,

Two sleepers at night lying close together as they sleep, one with an arm
    slanting down across and below the waist of the other,
The smell of apples, aromas from crush'd sage-plant, mint, birch-bark,
The boy's longings, the glow and pressure as he confides to me what he
    was dreaming,
The dead leaf whirling its spiral whirl and falling still and content
    to the ground,
The no-form'd stings that sights, people, objects, sting me with,
The hubb'd sting of myself, stinging me as much as it ever can any one,
The sensitive, orbic, underlapp'd brothers, that only privileged feelers may
    be intimate where they are,
The curious roamer the hand roaming all over the body, the bashful with-
    drawing of flesh where the fingers soothingly pause and edge themselves,
The limpid liquid within the young man,
The vex'd corrosion so pensive and so painful,
The torment, the irritable tide that will not be at rest,
The like of the same I feel, the like of the same in others,
The young man that flushes and flushes, and the young woman that flushes
    and flushes,
The young man that wakes deep at night, the hot hand seeking to repress
    what would master him,
The mystic amorous night, the strange half-welcome pangs, visions, sweats,
The pulse pounding through palms and trembling encircling fingers,
    the young man all color'd, red, ashamed, angry;
The souse upon me of my lover the sea, as I lie willing and naked,
The merriment of the twin babes that crawl over the grass in the sun,
    the mother never turning her vigilant eyes from them,

The walnut-trunk, the walnut-husks, and the ripening or ripen'd
    long-round walnuts,
The continence of vegetables, birds, animals,
The consequent meanness of me should I skulk or find myself indecent,
    while birds and animals never once skulk or find themselves indecent,
The great chastity of paternity, to match the great chastity of maternity,
The oath of procreation I have sworn, my Adamic and fresh daughters,
The greed that eats me day and night with hungry gnaw, till I saturate what
    shall produce boys to fill my place when I am through,
The wholesome relief, repose, content,
And this bunch pluck'd at random from myself,
It has done its work—I toss it carelessly to fall where it may.

MOMENTS

One of the Human Kinks

How is it that in all the serenity and lonesomeness of solitude, away off here amid the hush of the forest, alone, or as I have found in prairie wilds, or mountain stillness, one is never entirely without the instinct of looking around, (I never am, and others tell me the same of themselves, confidentially,) for somebody to appear, or start up out of the earth, or from behind some tree or rock? Is it a lingering, inherited remains of man's primitive wariness, from the wild animals? or from his savage ancestry far back? It is not at all nervousness or fear. Seems as if something unknown were possibly lurking in those bushes, or solitary places. Nay, it is quite certain there is—some vital unseen presence.

The Torch

On my Northwest coast in the midst of the night a fisherman's group
   stands watching,
Out on the lake that expands before them, others are spearing salmon,
The canoe, a dim shadowy thing, moves across the black water,
Bearing a torch ablaze at the prow.

A Farm Picture

Through the ample open door of the peaceful country barn,
A sunlit pasture field with cattle and horses feeding,
And haze and vista, and the far horizon fading away.

An Ulster County Waterfall

I jot this mem. in a wild scene of woods and hills, where we have come to visit a waterfall. I never saw finer or more copious hemlocks, many of them large, some old and hoary. Such a sentiment to them, secretive, shaggy—what I call weather-beaten and let-alone—a rich underlay of ferns, yew sprouts and mosses, beginning to be spotted with the early summer wild-flowers. Enveloping all, the monotone and liquid gurgle from the hoarse impetuous copious fall—the greenish-tawny, darkly transparent waters, plunging with velocity down the rocks, with patches of milk-white foam—a stream of hurrying amber, thirty feet wide, risen far back in the hills and woods, now rushing with volume—every hundred rods a fall, and sometimes three or four in that distance. A primitive forest, druidical, solitary and savage—not ten visitors a year— broken rocks everywhere—shade overhead, thick underfoot with leaves—a just palpable wild and delicate aroma.

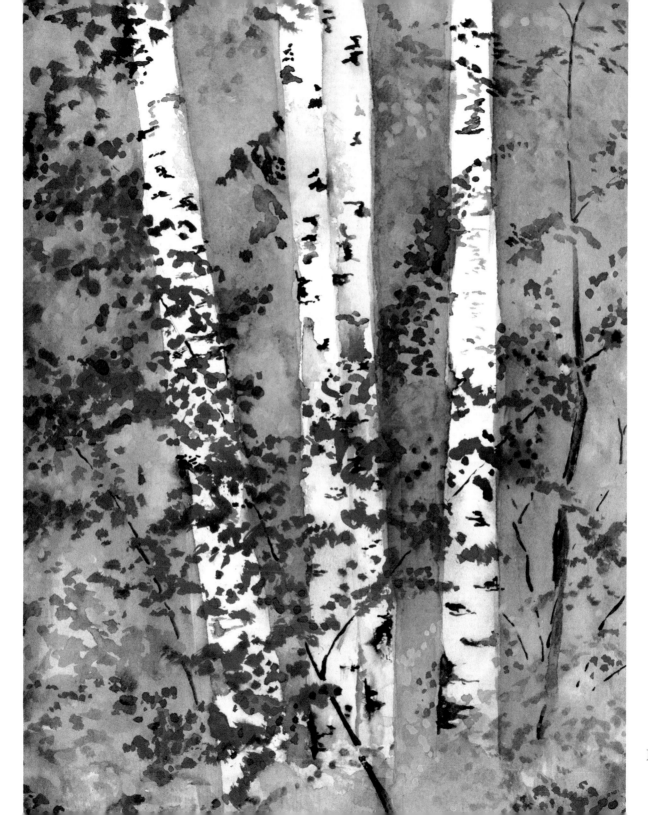

Seeing Niagara to Advantage

June 4, '80.—For really seizing a great picture or book, or piece of music, or architecture, or grand scenery—or perhaps for the first time even the common sunshine, or landscape, or may be even the mystery of identity, most curious mystery of all—there comes some lucky five minutes of a man's life, set amid a fortuitous concurrence of circumstances, and bringing in a brief flash the culmination of years of reading and travel and thought. The present case about two o'clock this afternoon, gave me Niagara, its superb severity of action and color and majestic grouping, in one short, indescribable show. We were very slowly crossing the Suspension bridge—not a full stop anywhere, but next to it—the day clear, sunny, still—and I out on the platform. The falls were in plain view about a mile off, but very distinct, and no roar—hardly a murmur. The river tumbling green and white, far below me; the dark high banks, the plentiful umbrage, many bronze cedars, in shadow; and tempering and arching all the immense materiality, a clear sky overhead, with a few white clouds, limpid, spiritual, silent. Brief, and as quiet as brief, that picture—a remembrance always afterwards. Such are the things, indeed, I lay away with my life's rare and blessed bits of hours, reminiscent, past—the wild sea-storm I once saw one winter day, off Fire island—the elder Booth in Richard, that famous night forty years ago in the old Bowery—or Alboni in the children's scene in Norma—or night-views, I remember, on the field, after battles in Virginia—or the peculiar sentiment of moonlight and stars over the great Plains, western Kansas—or scooting up New York bay, with a stiff breeze and a good yacht, off Navesink. With these, I say, I henceforth place that view, that afternoon, that combination complete, that five minutes' perfect absorption of Niagara—not the great majestic gem alone by itself, but set complete in all its varied, full, indispensable surroundings.

from Crossing Brooklyn Ferry

It avails not, time nor place—distance avails not,
I am with you, you men and women of a generation, or ever so many
  generations hence,
Just as you feel when you look on the river and sky, so I felt,
Just as any of you is one of a living crowd, I was one of a crowd,
Just as you are refresh'd by the gladness of the river and the bright
  flow, I was refresh'd,
Just as you stand and lean on the rail, yet hurry with the swift current,
  I stood yet was hurried,
Just as you look on the numberless masts of ships and the thick-
  stemm'd pipes of the steamboats, I look'd.

I too many and many a time cross'd the river of old,
Watched the Twelfth-month sea-gulls, saw them high in the air
  floating with motionless wings, oscillating their bodies,
Saw how the glistening yellow lit up parts of their bodies and left the
  rest in strong shadow,
Saw the reflection of the summer sky in the water,
Had my eyes dazzled by the shimmering track of beams,
Look'd at the fine centrifugal spokes of light round the shape of my
  head in the sunlit water . . .

from Our Old Feuillage

Evening—me in my room—the setting sun,
The setting summer sun shining in my open window, showing the swarm
    of flies, suspended, balancing in the air in the centre of the room, darting
    athwart, up and down, casting swift shadows in specks on the opposite
    wall where the shine is....

To the Sun-Set Breeze

Ah, whispering, something again, unseen,

Where late this heated day thou enterest at my window, door,

Thou, laving, tempering all, cool-refreshing, gently vitalizing

Me, old, alone, sick, weak-down, melted-worn with sweat;

Thou, nestling, folding close and firm yet soft, companion better than talk,
    book, art,

(Thou hast, O Nature! elements! utterance to my heart beyond the rest—
    and this is of them,)

So sweet thy primitive taste to breathe within—thy soothing fingers on
    my face and hands,

Thou, messenger-magical strange bringer to body and spirit of me,

(Distances balk'd—occult medicines penetrating me from head to foot,)

I feel the sky, the prairies vast—I feel the mighty northern lakes,

I feel the ocean and the forest—somehow I feel the globe itself swift-
    swimming in space;

Thou blown from lips so loved, now gone—haply from the endless store,
    God-sent,

(For thou art spiritual, Godly, most of all known to my sense,)

Minister to speak to me, here and now, what word has never told, and
    cannot tell,

Art thou not universal concrete's distillation? Law's, all Astronomy's
    last refinement?

Hast thou no soul? Can I not know, identify thee?

Distant Sounds

The axe of the wood-cutter, the measured thud of a single threshing-flail, the crowing of chanticleer in the barn-yard, (with invariable responses from the other barn-yards,) and the lowing of cattle—but most of all, or far or near, the wind—through the high tree-tops, or through low bushes, laving one's face and hands gently, this balmy-bright noon, the coolest for a long time, (Sept. 2)—I will not call it *sighing*, for to me it is always a firm, sane, cheery expression, though a monotone, giving many varieties, or swift or slow, or dense or delicate. The wind in the patch of pine woods off there—how sibilant. Or at sea, I can imagine it this moment, tossing the waves, with spirts of foam flying far, and the free whistle, and the scent of the salt—and that vast paradox somehow with all its action and restlessness conveying a sense of eternal rest.

NIGHT SKIES

When I Heard the Learn'd Astronomer

When I heard the learn'd astronomer,
When the proofs, the figures, were ranged in columns before me,
When I was shown the charts and diagrams, to add, divide, and
   measure them,
When I sitting heard the astronomer where he lectured with much
   applause in the lecture-room,
How soon unaccountable I became tired and sick,
Till rising and gliding out I wander'd off by myself,
In the mystical moist night-air, and from time to time,
Look'd up in perfect silence at the stars.

from Hours for the Soul

THE MOON.—*May 18.*—I went to bed early last night, but found myself waked shortly after 12, and, turning awhile sleepless and mentally feverish, I rose, dress'd myself, sallied forth and walk'd down the lane. The full moon, some three or four hours up—a sprinkle of light and less-light clouds just lazily moving—Jupiter an hour high in the east, and here and there throughout the heavens a random star appearing and disappearing. So, beautifully veil'd and varied—the air, with that early-summer perfume, not at all damp or raw—at times Luna languidly emerging in richest brightness for minutes, and then

partially envelop'd again. Far off a whip-poor-will plied his notes incessantly. It was that silent time between 1 and 3. . . .

Furthermore.—*February 19, 1880.*—Just before 10 P.M. cold and entirely clear again, the show overhead, bearing southwest, of wonderful and crowded magnificence. The moon in her third quarter—the clusters of the Hyades and Pleiades, with the planet Mars between—in full crossing sprawl in the sky the great Egyptian X, (Sirius, Procyon, and the main stars in the constellations of the Ship, the Dove, and of Orion;) just north of east Bootes, and in his knee Arcturus, an hour high, mounting the heaven, ambitiously large and sparkling, as if he meant to challenge with Sirius the stellar supremacy.

With the sentiment of the stars and moon such nights I get all the free margins and indefiniteness of music or poetry, fused in geometry's utmost exactness.

154

Full-Starr'd Nights

May 21.—Back in Camden. Again commencing one of those unusually transparent, full-starr'd, blue-black nights, as if to show that however lush and pompous the day may be, there is something left in the not-day that can outvie it. The rarest, finest sample of long-drawn-out clear-obscure, from sundown to 9 o'clock. I went down to the Delaware, and cross'd and cross'd. Venus like blazing silver well up in the west. The large pale thin crescent of the new moon, half an hour high, sinking languidly under a bar-sinister of cloud, and then emerging. Arcturus right overhead. A faint fragrant sea-odor wafted up from the south. The gloaming, the temper'd coolness, with every feature of the scene, indescribably soothing and tonic—one of those hours that give hints to the soul, impossible to put in a statement. (Ah, where would be any food for spirituality without night and the stars?) The vacant spaciousness of the air, and the veil'd blue of the heavens, seem'd miracles enough.

As the night advanc'd it changed its spirit and garments to ampler stateliness. I was almost conscious of a definite presence, Nature silently near. The great constellation of the Water-Serpent stretch'd its coils over more than half the heavens. The Swan with outspread wings was flying down the Milky Way. The northern Crown, the Eagle, Lyra, all up there in their places. From the whole dome shot down points of light, rapport with me, through the clear blue-black. All the usual sense of motion, all animal life, seem'd discarded, seem'd a fiction; a curious power, like the placid rest of Egyptian gods, took possession, none the less potent for being impalpable. Earlier I had seen many bats, balancing in the luminous twilight, darting their black forms hither and yon over the river; but now they altogether disappear'd. The evening star and the moon had gone. Alertness and peace lay calmly couching together through the fluid universal shadows.

Bivouac on a Mountain Side

I see before me now a traveling army halting,
Below a fertile valley spread, with barns and the orchards of summer,
Behind, the terraced sides of a mountain, abrupt, in places rising high,
Broken, with rocks, with clinging cedars, with tall shapes dingily seen,
The numerous camp-fires scatter'd near and far, some away up
    on the mountain,
The shadowy forms of men and horses, looming, large-sized, flickering,
And over all the sky—the sky! far, far out of reach, studded, breaking out,
    the eternal stars.

Look Down Fair Moon

Look down fair moon and bathe this scene,
Pour softly down night's nimbus floods on faces ghastly, swollen, purple,
On the dead on their backs with arms toss'd wide,
Pour down your unstinted nimbus sacred moon.

A Silent Night Ramble

October 20th.—To-night, after leaving the hospital at 10 o'clock, (I had been on self-imposed duty some five hours, pretty closely confined,) I wander'd a long time around Washington. The night was sweet, very clear, sufficiently cool, a voluptuous half-moon, slightly golden, the space near it of a transparent blue-gray tinge. I walk'd up Pennsylvania avenue, and then to Seventh street, and a long while around the Patent-office. Some-how it look'd rebukefully strong, majestic, there in the delicate moonlight. The sky, the planets, the constellations all so bright, so calm, so expressively silent, so soothing, after those hospital scenes. I wander'd to and fro till the moist moon set, long after midnight.

Hours for the Soul

July 22d, 1878.—Living down in the country again. A wonderful conjunction of all that goes to make those sometime miracle-hours after sunset—so near and yet so far. Perfect, or nearly perfect days, I notice, are not so very uncommon; but the combinations that make perfect nights are few, even in a life time. We have one of those perfections to-night. Sunset left things pretty clear; the larger stars were visible soon as the shades allow'd. A while after 8, three or four great black clouds suddenly rose, seemingly from different points, and sweeping with broad swirls of wind but no thunder, underspread the orbs from view everywhere, and indicated a violent heat-storm. But without storm, clouds, blackness and all, sped and vanish'd as suddenly as they had risen; and from a little after 9 till 11 the atmosphere and the whole show above were in that state of exceptional clearness and glory just alluded to. In the northwest turned the Great Dipper with its pointers round the Cynosure. A little south of east the constellation of the Scorpion was fully up, with red Antares glowing in its neck; while dominating, majestic Jupiter swam, an hour and a half risen, in the east—(no moon till after 11.) A large part of the sky seem'd just laid in great splashes of phosphorous. You could look deeper in, farther through, than usual; the orbs thick as heads of wheat in a field. Not that there was any special brilliancy either—nothing near as sharp as I have seen of keen winter nights, but a curious general luminousness throughout to sight, sense, and soul. The latter had much to do with it. (I am convinced there are hours of Nature, especially of the atmosphere, mornings and evenings, address'd to the soul. Night transcends, for that purpose, what the proudest day can do.) Now, indeed, if never before, the heavens declared the glory of God. It was to the full the sky of the Bible, of Arabia, of the prophets, and of the oldest poems. There, in abstraction and stillness, (I had gone off by myself to absorb the scene, to have the spell unbroken,) the copiousness, the removedness, vitality, loose-clear-crowdedness, of that stellar concave spreading overhead, softly absorb'd into me, rising so free, interminably high, stretching east, west, north, south—and I, though but a point in the centre below, embodying all.

As if for the first time, indeed, creation noiselessly sank into and through me its placid and untellable lesson, beyond—O, so infinitely beyond!—anything from art, books, sermons, or from science, old or new. The spirit's hour—religion's hour—the visible suggestion of God in space and time—now once definitely indicated, if never again. The untold pointed at—the heavens all paved with it. The Milky Way, as if some superhuman symphony, some ode of universal vagueness, disdaining syllable and sound—the flashing glance of Deity, address'd to the soul. All silently—the indescribable night and stars—far off and silently.

A Clear Midnight

This is thy hour O Soul, thy free flight into the wordless,
Away from books, away from art, the day erased, the lesson done,
Thee fully forth emerging, silent, gazing, pondering the themes
    thou lovest best,
Night, sleep, death and the stars.

THINKING and SINGING about the EARTH

The Common Earth, the Soil

The soil, too—let others pen-and-ink the sea, the air, (as I sometimes try)—but now I feel to choose the common soil for theme—naught else. The brown soil here, (just between winter-close and opening spring and vegetation)—the rain-shower at night, and the fresh smell next morning—the red worms wriggling out of the ground—the dead leaves, the incipient grass, and the latent life underneath—the effort to start something—already in shelter'd spots some little flowers—the distant emerald show of winter wheat and the rye-fields—the yet naked trees, with clear interstices, giving prospects hidden in summer—the tough fallow and the plow-team, and the stout boy whistling to his horses for encouragement—and there the dark fat earth in long slanting stripes upturn'd.

A Thought of the Clef of Eternity

What can the future bring me more than I have?
Do you suppose I wish to enjoy life in other spheres?

I say distinctly I comprehend no better sphere than this earth,
I comprehend no better life than the life of my body.

I do not know what follows the death of my body,
But I know well that whatever it is, it is best for me,
And I know well that whatever is really Me shall live just as much as before.

I am not uneasy but I shall have good housing to myself,
But this is my first—how can I like the rest any better?
Here I grew up—the studs and rafters are grown parts of me.

I am not uneasy but I am to be beloved by young and old men, and to love
    them the same,
I suppose the pink nipples of the breasts of women with whom I shall sleep
    will touch the side of my face the same,
But this is the nipple of a breast of my mother, always near and always divine
    to me, her true child and son, whatever comes.

I suppose I am to be eligible to visit the stars, in my time,
I suppose I shall have myriads of new experiences—and that the experience
    of this earth will prove only one out of myriads;
But I believe my body and my Soul already indicate those experiences,
And I believe I shall find nothing in the stars more majestic and beautiful
    than I have already found on the earth,
And I believe I have this night a clew through the universes,
And I believe I have this night thought a thought of the clef of eternity.

Thinking and Singing about the Earth

from A Song of Joys

O for the voices of animals—O for the swiftness and balance of fishes!
O for the dropping of raindrops in a song!
O for the sunshine and motion of waves in a song!

Birds—and a Caution

May 14.—Home again; down temporarily in the Jersey woods. Between 8 and 9 A.M. a full concert of birds, from different quarters, in keeping with the fresh scent, the peace, the naturalness all around me. I am lately noticing the russet-back, size of the robin or a trifle less, light breast and shoulders, with irregular dark stripes—tail long—sits hunch'd up by the hour these days, top of a tall bush, or some tree, singing blithely. I often get near and listen, as he seems tame; I like to watch the working of his bill and throat, the quaint sidle of his body, and flex of his long tail. I hear the woodpecker, and night and early morning the shuttle of the whip-poor-will—noons, the gurgle of thrush delicious, and *meo-o-ow* of the cat-bird. Many I cannot name; but I do not particularly seek information. (You must not know too much, or be too precise or scientific about birds and trees and flowers and water-craft; a certain free margin, and even vagueness—perhaps ignorance, credulity—helps your enjoyment of these things, and of the sentiment of feather'd, wooded, river, or marine Nature generally. I repeat it—don't want to know too exactly, or the reasons why. My own notes have been written off-hand in the latitude of middle New Jersey. Though they describe what I saw—what appear'd to me—I dare say the expert ornithologist, botanist or entomologist will detect more than one slip in them.)

from A Song of the Rolling Earth

The earth does not argue,
Is not pathetic, has no arrangements,
Does not scream, haste, persuade, threaten, promise,
Makes no discriminations, has no conceivable failures,
Closes nothing, refuses nothing, shuts none out,
Of all the powers, objects, states, it notifies, shuts none out.

The earth does not exhibit itself nor refuse to exhibit itself,
    possesses still underneath,
Underneath the ostensible sounds, the august chorus of heroes,
    the wail of slaves,
Persuasions of lovers, curses, gasps of the dying, laughter of
    young people, accents of bargainers,
Underneath these possessing words that never fail.

To her children the words of the eloquent dumb great mother
    never fail,
The true words do not fail, for motion does not fail and reflection
    does not fail,
Also the day and night do not fail, and the voyage we pursue
    does not fail.

Earth, My Likeness

November 8, '76

The forenoon leaden and cloudy, not cold or wet, but indicating both. As I hobble down here and sit by the silent pond, how different from the excitement amid which, in the cities, millions of people are now waiting news of yesterday's Presidential election, or receiving and discussing the result—in this secluded place uncared-for, unknown.

Thinking and Singing about the Earth

The Calming Thought of All

That coursing on, whate'er men's speculations,
Amid the changing schools, theologies, philosophies,
Amid the bawling presentations new and old,
The round earth's silent vital laws, facts, modes continue.

from Song at Sunset

Good in all,
In the satisfaction and aplomb of animals,
In the annual return of the seasons,
In the hilarity of youth,
In the strength and flush of manhood,
In the grandeur and exquisiteness of old age,
In the superb vistas of death.

Wonderful to depart!
Wonderful to be here!
The heart, to jet the all-alike and innocent blood!
To breathe the air, how delicious!
To speak—to walk—to seize something by the hand!
To prepare for sleep, for bed, to look on my rose-color'd flesh!
To be conscious of my body, so satisfied, so large!
To be this incredible God I am!
To have gone forth among other Gods, these men and women I love.

Wonderful how I celebrate you and myself!
How my thoughts play subtly at the spectacles around!
How the clouds pass silently overhead!
How the earth darts on and on! and how the sun, moon, stars, dart
    on and on!
How the water sports and sings! (surely it is alive!)
How the trees rise and stand up, with strong trunks, with branches
    and leaves!
(Surely there is something more in each of the trees, some living soul.)

A July Afternoon by the Pond

The fervent heat, but so much more endurable in this pure air—the white and pink pond-blossoms, with great heart-shaped leaves; the glassy waters of the creek, the banks, with dense bushery, and the picturesque beeches and shade and turf; the tremulous, reedy call of some bird from recesses, breaking the warm, indolent, half-voluptous silence; an occasional wasp, hornet, honey-bee or bumble (they hover near my hands or face, yet annoy me not, nor I them, as they appear to examine, find nothing, and away they go)—the vast space of the sky overhead so clear, and the buzzard up there sailing his slow whirl in majestic spirals and discs; just over the surface of the pond, two large slate-color'd dragon-flies, with wings of lace, circling and darting and occasionally balancing themselves quite still, their wings quivering all the time, (are they not showing off for my amusement?)—the pond itself, with the sword-shaped calamus; the water snakes—occasionally a flitting blackbird, with red dabs on his shoulders, as he darts slantingly by—the sounds that bring out the solitude, warmth, light and shade—the quawk of some pond duck—(the crickets and grasshoppers are mute in the noon heat, but I hear the song of the first cicadas;)—then at some distance the rattle and whirr of a reaping machine as the horses draw it on a rapid walk through a rye field on the opposite side of the creek—(what was the yellow or light-brown bird, large as a young hen, with short neck and long-stretch'd legs I just saw, in flapping and awkward flight over there through the trees?)—the prevailing delicate, yet palpable, spicy, grassy, clovery perfume to my nostrils; and over all, encircling all, to my sight and soul, the free space of the sky, transparent and blue—and hovering there in the west, a mass of white-gray fleecy clouds the sailors call "shoals of mackerel"—the sky, with silver like locks of toss'd hair, spreading, expanding—a vast voiceless, formless simulacrum—yet may-be the most real reality and formulator of everything—who knows?

Thinking and Singing about the Earth

175

Earth, My Likeness

from Song of Myself

The spotted hawk swoops by and accuses me, he complains
   of my gab and my loitering.

I too am not a bit tamed, I too am untranslatable,
I sound my barbaric yawp over the roofs of the world.

The last scud of day holds back for me,
It flings my likeness after the rest and true as any on the
   shadow'd wilds,
It coaxes me to the vapor and the dusk.

I depart as air, I shake my white locks at the runaway sun,
I effuse my flesh in eddies, and drift it in lacy jags.

I bequeath myself to the dirt to grow from the grass I love,
If you want me again look for me under your boot-soles.

You will hardly know who I am or what I mean,
But I shall be good health to you nevertheless,
And filter and fibre your blood.

Failing to fetch me at first keep encouraged,
Missing me one place search another,
I stop somewhere waiting for you.

List of Illustrations

All the watercolors in this book are by Roderick MacIver, founder of Heron Dance. Select watercolors from this list are available as full-color, limited-edition prints on the Heron Dance Web site (www.herondance.org) by typing the title in the search bar. If you have trouble finding the image you would like or do not have access to the Internet, please call Heron Dance toll-free at 888-304-3766 or send an e-mail to heron@herondance.org. Thank you.

Heron Dance

Heron Dance Press & Art Studio is a nonprofit 501(c)(3) organization founded in 1995.

Heron Dance explores the beauty and mystery of the natural world through art and words. It is a work of love, an effort to produce something that is thought-provoking and beautiful. We offer *A Pause for Beauty, The Heron Dance Nature Art Journal*, and note cards, books, and calendars.

We invite you to visit us at www.herondance.org to view the hundreds of watercolors by Roderick MacIver and to browse the hundreds of pages of book excerpts, poetry, essays, and interviews of authors and artists.

Nonprofit Donations

Heron Dance donates thousands of note cards and the use of hundreds of images to small nonprofits every year. We also donate books and prints for fundraisers. Please contact us for more information.

The Heron Dance Nature Art Journal

Available by subscription, *The Heron Dance Nature Art Journal* is a 72-page full-color journal published twice a year that features nature watercolors by Roderick MacIver throughout. In its latest incarnation, it is a semi-fictional account of a wild artist who loves wild places, wild rivers, and wild women. It is a celebration of the gift of life! Visit our Web site to get more information (click Subscribe or Renew) and to sign up.

Our Free Weekly E-newsletter: *A Pause for Beauty*

Each issue features a new watercolor or acrylic ink painting, and a poem, quotation, or reflection. Over 25,000 people have signed up for *A Pause for Beauty*. To sign up or view our archives, please visit our Web site.

Watercolors by Roderick MacIver

Hundreds of nature watercolors are available as signed limited-edition prints and originals at www.herondance.org.

Online Gallery

We offer note cards, daybooks, calendars, address books, and blank journals that feature Roderick MacIver watercolors, along with inspirational titles from HERON DANCE Press, including *The Heron Dance Book of Love and Gratitude*.

HERON DANCE Community

The HERON DANCE community consists of over 12,000 subscribers to our print journal and over 25,000 readers of our free weekly e-mail *A Pause for Beauty*. To connect with other Heron Dancers, please visit our Facebook page. Links to that page and to founder Rod MacIver's page can be found by going to the HERON DANCE Web site, then clicking About HERON DANCE and then Connect with Other Heron Dancers.

- www.herondance.org
- 802-922-9652
- heron@herondance.org

About the Editor

Photo by E. Bruce Walter

HOWARD NELSON is Professor of English at Cayuga Community College and has been awarded Chancellor's Awards from the State University of New York for teaching and for scholarship and creative activities. Nelson is a widely published poet, whose latest collection, *The Nap by the Waterfall*, was published by Timberline Press in 2009. He has also written critical studies of American poetry including *Robert Bly: An Introduction to the Poetry* and *On the Poetry of Galway Kinnell: The Wages of Dying*. Nelson is contributing editor to *The Hollins Critic*, where many of his essays and reviews have appeared. A long-time student of nineteenth-century American literature, he has a special interest in Walt Whitman and was a contributor to the *Walt Whitman Encyclopedia* and *The Walt Whitman Companion*. Nelson, who lives in Moravia, New York, was keynote speaker at the celebration of Whitman's birthday at the Whitman House in Camden, New Jersey, in 2008. He reads his poetry and lectures on Whitman and other American writers regularly.

About the Artist

ODERICK MACIVER is a Canadian-born watercolor artist whose artwork has been acquired by public and private collectors. He has donated thousands of his images to grassroots wilderness protection groups and these organizations, along with other nonprofits, have used his art in their newsletters, on their Web sites, and in their outreach efforts. In 1995 he founded Heron Dance (herondance.org), a nonprofit organization that celebrates the human connection to nature through art and words. His own words and watercolors are inspired by a love of wild places and the peace and rhythm he finds there. MacIver, who currently resides in Vermont, is a person of curious mind, of major strengths and major weaknesses, of contradictions and integrity. He has fought forest fires in northern Canada with Dogrib Indians, worked as a Wall Street investment analyst, lived with cancer, and engaged in a serious spiritual search.